Real Estate Investing

How to invest successfully in Real Estate & How to Flip Houses for Passive Income & How to become a successful Real Estate Agent

By Sabi Shepherd

Table of Contents

Part 1 - Real Estate Investing For Beginners

How to invest successfully in Real Estate

By Sabi Shepherd

Introduction

Investing your money is probably one of the smartest things that you can do to help it grow and to set yourself up for a life of financial security. When it comes to investments though, there are a lot of options you can make. Some people choose to get into the stock market and hope that they make the right predictions while others are more interested in starting a business, working on their retirement plan, or using another of the many methods. But one option for investing that is growing in popularity is real estate investing.

Real estate investing is a great option because there are so many choices that you can make and since it is not a one size fits all, you will be able to see results on your own time and by trying something new. You can choose to purchase a small home or apartment building and make money from renting it out to others. Some are interested in purchasing a home, making some changes, and flipping it. And still others will do a great job at sniffing out the deals and then will sell the deeds to the property to someone else before even holding onto the actual property. As you can see, the possibilities are endless.

This guidebook is going to spend time talking about real estate investing and all it has to offer. As a beginner, it is common to have questions and concerns about how to get started and this guidebook aims to help you understand what this investment is all about. We will start out with some of the basics of real estate investing before moving into some of the strategies that you can try for success, how to find financing, finding your first help out. Rental properties will need upkeep and when it is time to find a new tenant, you will have to do the legwork. Flipping houses requires maintenance, fixing things, and hoping that the house sells quickly.

Even with the work, real estate investing can be worth the time. For the smart investor, it opens the opportunity to make a lot of money quickly. You need to be good at catching deals and getting homes for really good discounts and ideally only having to put a small amount of money in them before turning a profit. This doesn't always happen, especially for the beginner investor, but it is something that you can work towards.

The issue with real estate investing is that beginners feel they can just purchase a property and sell it in a few days without any issues. Unfortunately, this is not how the process works. Most homes will need more than a little bit of work and unless you got the property for way under market value, it is going to sit on the market for sale for some time. During this time, you are not just paying for any repairs you make, but also for the utilities, taxes, insurance, closing costs and more. Failure to predict these costs or assuming they won't be that bad is the reason that many people end up failing in this business.

The good news is that this leaves a lot of room open for those who are serious about getting into real estate. You have to be good at planning, know how to keep your expenses down, and learn how to find the best deals so you can actually make a profit. But when it all comes together, you will find that real estate investing can be a really rewarding investment.

How to make money in real estate

The first question that you may ask is how people make money with real estate investing. Obviously most people will think about house flippers who purchase a home, make some changes, and then try to sell it for a profit. And others may think of landlords who purchase properties and then rent them out to others to make a profit each month. While these are two forms of earning with real estate investing, they are not the only options. Some other ways that people have made money with real estate include:

Real estate appreciation

For this option, the property will need to become more valuable a year or so down the line, simply because there are going to be changes in the market. This sometimes happens when there is a downturn in the economy. Families may have to sell their homes for less, but there may be some rumors of big changes that would drive the market back up again, such as a new sports center or other big business coming in and offering new jobs. This would drive the price of the home up with very little work on the investors part.

There are a few things that have to happen here though. First, the investor needs to be pretty certain that the real estate market will go up in the next year or so. It is important to do your research and not just go on some rumors about the change or you could be stuck with a property and very little to show for it. In addition, you need to be able to afford to make the monthly mortgage payments, plus insurance and taxes, for a year or so until the home is sold.

Cash flow income

With the cash flow income, the investor will purchase a property, such as a single family home or apartment building, and then rent it out to someone else. Apartment buildings are often the ones that provide the biggest cash flow since there are many tenants there, but they do have higher turnaround rates where you will have to spend a lot of time with empty spaces and having to search for new tenants. This is why duplexes and single family homes are more popular since the stream of income is steadier.

This is a great investment opportunity if you are looking to create that income while still holding onto the property. With luck they may be in pretty good shape when you make the purchase, just needing a few minor updates, and then you can rent them out to someone else. Keep in mind that as the landlord, you will be responsible for maintenance and taking care of the property.

Real estate income

This one will work more on commission and you usually don't own the property. These require specialists who may run the property for the owners and then will take some of the commission that is earned. For example, a real estate management company will help to run various rental properties for the landlord and will receive some of the rents for doing this work. If you are looking for a way to get into the real estate market and learn a bit more about upkeep and maintenance of homes, this could be a good place to start.

Ancillary real estate income

For this option, you will already own a property and are most likely renting it out. Apartment buildings are the ones who will use ancillary income the most. They are added into the mix to give the landlord a bit more income while also providing a convenience for the tenants. Examples of this kind of income include vending machines and laundry facilities. When these are located inside the apartment building, it can really bring in some more money because tenants are more likely to use the ones closest to them, rather than going somewhere else to get a snack or do their laundry.

Understanding the real estate market

When you are considering getting into real estate, it is important to gain a good understanding of the whole market. There are always going to be homes that are on the market, but not all of them are going to help you get a good profit. Depending on the time of year, the amount that you pay on the property, and even the economy at the time will all influence how much, if anything, you are going to make on your investment.

This is going to take some research before you even get started. You need to understand a number of things including;

- If the market is good—if the market is in a downturn, interest rates have gone up, or there is an issue with layoffs and downturns in the area you want to invest, it may not be a good time to get started because no one will purchase the property. If you are able to hold onto the property for a bit, or use it as a rental property, it may be worth your time to consider if you're sure the market will go back up since you can get some good deals.

- Find the good areas—you need to recognize where the hot areas in town are. You should look around school districts and some of the newer constructions. Sometimes homes will pop up here at great discounts and you can make some minor changes to earn the investment.

- Prices—look at the prices in your area and find out what is normal. If you find a home that is offered for a lower price in a nice area, and there isn't much wrong with it, it may be worth your time to look into.

- Consider the area—the area you purchase the home will make a big difference on how well this goes. For example, it is easier to sell a home that is near the schools or other popular areas than it is to sell one that is outside of town (unless it is on a big acreage).

Looking at the real estate market will take some time and an eye for detail. Beginners often get aught up in the moment and want to make money quickly. They may not take into account how different market conditions, the location, and more will influence how they are able to sell the house. This is why many don't make it very far in real estate, but with a bit of research, finding a good mentor to help you along the way, and some good thinking skills, it is possible to do well in real estate.

Getting the Right Financing

Getting the right financing is often considered one of the hardest parts to getting started. Most people are not going to have all the money they need to purchase the whole house upfront and make any necessary adjustments. This means that to get started with real estate investing, you will have to go talk to a bank, credit union, or other source to figure out how much you are able to afford and to get through all the steps to purchase that property.

You will find when you first start applying for your mortgage that banks and other lending sources are stricter for real estate investments than what you will find for those who are purchasing the home for personal use. This is because the banks worry that you will not succeed and they want to make sure they get as much money back as possible. You will notice that the financing terms are harder, the interest rates are higher, and you are much more likely to get turned down for real estate investment funding than for your regular mortgage.

Luckily, there are a few things that you will be able to do that help increase the chances of getting funding. First, make sure that your personal finances are all in order. Just like with a regular mortgage, if your credit score, bills, debts, and other financial information is all over the place, it is impossible to get the funding. You should also try to get some sort of down payment together assuage the lender. Never stick with just one lender when you start out because there are often variances in the rates and deals you can get from different lenders and shopping around can be beneficial.

Choosing the Right Property

Once you have taken some time to research the market and find out what some of your options are for funding, it is a good idea to figure out what kind of property you would like to invest in. Most of the time, it is connected to your personal goals. For example, if you want to get into land investing, you will want to look for a good area of land to purchase and hold onto until it is worth more. If you want to do rental properties, it is important to find a good home in a nice area to make money from. Figure out your goals and you will find that it is much easier to discover your perfect property.

The biggest thing that you must remember no matter what you are doing with real estate is to take it slow. Those who rush into the whole process without some good thinking and research are the ones who end up failing in the long run. Start out with just a few buildings, even if you want to run an empire, and get a feel for the whole market. You will always be able to build up some more later, but it is nice to have a starting point you can learn from and also handle.

Updating the property

Once you own the property, it is time to get working on the updates that will increase the value. There are two ways that you can go about this. When renting out the property, you need to make sure that you are making the home livable, comfortable, and appealing to a wide range of people. You will not need to do quite as many updates with a rental property since you aren't trying to convince the tenants to purchase the home, but a few updates can make the home more appealing and will ensure that a new tenant will come in soon and be willing to pay your rates.

When it comes to flipping a home, you may need to do a few more updates. These updates need to convince the potential buyer that they want your house and not another one without costing you too much. Simple things like a new paint job, fixing a few things that are broken, and even improving thc lights can make a big difference when the buyers come to look.

Selling the home

After all the updates are done on the home, it is time to start making the profits. You will need to start posting information about the property to potential renters and buyers so you can start making money on the property before another mortgage payment is due.

For renting, posting online, in the newspaper, and with billboards will help potential tenants know that the property is available. You will want to make sure that you offer a competitive rent price so that you make as much as possible but you aren't turning renters away because the price is too high for the area.

Selling the property can take even more effort in some cases. You need to convince a potential buyer that the property is worth at least as much as you are asking and this sometimes takes a few months before someone is interested. In addition, there is a lot of paperwork that comes with selling a home. Hiring a realtor can really help out with all these steps as a beginner.

Moving on to the next project

Once you have either built up some rental money from the property or sold a home you were planning on flipping, it is time to move on to your next project. If you did well with this one, the second time around may be a bit easier. You can use some of your profits as a down payment on the next property and since you already worked with the bank, you will be able to work with them again and have an easier time with getting more funding for the next project. Make sure to follow all the same steps when picking out the second, third, and so on projects and you will soon see this business grow.

Real estate investing can be one of the most rewarding sources of investing. You get to make the choices, picking the type of property you would like to use, how many hours you want to put into the project, and even the type of work that you want to do within real estate. And when it all comes together, you can easily realize a great profit.

Chapter 2: Strategies and Options When Investing in Real Estate

With some of the basics of real estate investing understood, it is time to go over some of the strategies that you should have when going into real estate. This is an investment and just like with any good form of investing, you need to have a plan and know how you are going to get things done. Often it will depend on the goals that you have in place for your business, such as wanting to get a big empire of apartment building for a big income or just wanting to do this on the side to make some extra money. Here we will look at some of your options when creating your real estate strategy.

Choosing the Niche

The first thing that you should do is decide what niche you want to have in real estate. As a beginner, you should only choose one of these niches because you don't want to take on more than you can handle. Luckily, there are a lot of different niches that you can go with in real estate so picking one shouldn't be too difficult.

Raw land

Raw land is one of the first places that you can start with real estate investing. When you invest in raw land, you are basically just purchasing some land, usually without anything on it, that no one else owns. You may be able to do some things with the land to improve it, such as adding an orchard or combining a few plots and selling it as one. Some will choose to purchase raw land and then build a home there to sell.

To be successful with investing in raw land, you need to know that the prices of land are about to go up. In most economies, raw land is going to stay pretty steady so if you aren't careful, you are not going to get much more than you paid for the land. But if you are in an area that is growing rapidly or there are some developments that arc coming to the area, snatching up some raw land early on could set you up for a big profit when someone else wants that land.

Single family homes

Most first time investors will stick with single family homes. There is a lot of diversification when it comes to these homes, but they are still simple enough that most beginners can handle them. You can make a few different decisions with this kind of home, such as using it as a rental property or flipping it, and it is easy to make changes if one of the options is not working for you.

Duplexes

If you are looking to get more into the rental side of things and want to increase your income more than what a single family home can provide, going with duplexes can still be a great place to start as a beginner. These will usually hold four to eight units, enough that you are making a bigger income but small enough that you aren't going to be so overwhelmed. These usually still have a pretty low turnover rate of tenants so most of them will stay put for some time, making the income stream steady and saving you time and money from having to advertise all the time. It is a great middle road to help you build your portfolio and gain more experience before moving up further.

Apartments

Next on the list are apartments. These are a great way to make some big money, but you have to remember that they are a lot of work. You have to maintain them, advertise for vacancies (and there can be a lot of these in apartment buildings) and hope that you get enough rent to keep up with the costs. Many landlords of bigger apartment complexes will also higher a management team to help them keep up with the demands, something that is useful but which will take more out of your profit.

For the most part, apartments are not the best option for the beginner to start out with. They take a lot of time and can quickly lose money if you don't know what you are doing. Sure, they can make you quite a bit of money, but it is best to get your feet wet a bit with single family homes and duplexes before jumping into this project.

Commercial Properties

Another option that most beginner investors don't consider but which could yield a good amount of money are commercial real estate properties. This investment style is when you purchase a property that can be used by businesses. There are many options that come with commercial properties and you can choose between big megastores or small businesses, different styles and sizes, and so much more. The biggest drawback is that when a tenant leaves, it is sometimes hard to find a new one, but once you have a tenant, they will usually stay around for a long time to come.

Buy and Hold

One strategy that you can use in real estate is the buy and hold. This is going to allow you to purchase the property and then hold onto it. For the most part, you will rent it out to someone else or make money in another way on the property while still being the one who owns the building. This is a great way to get cash flow from the rent and you are still paying down the mortgage. You could rent out for a few years while making some changes and then have more equity in the home for other projects or be able to make a bigger profit when you sell the home.

Don't just jump into this opportunity though. People are not going to rent a home that is in disarray or which needs a lot of work. You need to find a property that is in good working order, or won't take much work to get it there, and will also fit into your budget without making rent too high. As the landlord, you will be responsible for any maintenance and issues that come up with the home since you are the owner. At times, the property could be vacant between tenants and you will still need to pay the mortgage as well as for advertising the vacancy.

While there are some drawbacks to this opportunity, those who are able to manage the properties well and keep the tenant happy will be able to make a steady income while still leaving the door open for other opportunities later on.

Flipping Homes

One of the most popular options for beginners in real estate is flipping homes. They may have seen some popular television shows or heard of someone who became rich when flipping a home and now they want to get in on the action. And while it is true that there is the possibility to make a lot of money with flipping homes, it is important to remember that you will need to put in a lot of work and often the profits won't be as big as advertised.

Still flipping homes can be lucrative if you know what you are doing. When flipping a home, you are going to find a property that is discounted before making some updates or riding out the market a bit and then selling it for a higher price. This sounds simple in theory, but there is so much more to it. Finding a home that is discounted at a good price that won't take years of time and hard earned money to fix up is hard, and sometimes selling a home can take a long time too.

As an investor, you need to learn how to make the hard decisions. You need to be able to determine if the home really is a good deal at the discounted price, or are you going to spend more time, energy, and money on the home than it is worth. If the home really is a good discount and there are just some minor things that would make it easier to sell, then go for it and start on the project. But if it needs a lot of work and you will waste your life fixing it up, it may be best to pass on that property.

When picking a property, keep in mind that speed is important. If you are not able to get the upkeep and fixes done within a few months, is it really worth your time? Not only are you paying for all the fixes during this time, but you have to pay for insurance, mortgage payments, taxes, and more. This is in addition to the time you will need to make those payments while the property is on the market waiting to sell. You will have to decide whether the property is worth all this extra money and hassle or not.

Wholesale Real Estate

This is another strategy that most beginners, and even some who have been in the industry for some time, may not consider. With wholesaling, you are basically finding a good deal in the market, writing out a contract for that deal, and then selling the contract to someone else. The wholesaler will usually never even own the property, but they will get it to the point of being under contract and then sell that contract with a fee attached.

This is a lucrative way to make some money without ever having to own the property or worrying about whether the property is selling or not. Some have made $5000 or more depending on the property and how high in demand it is. You are basically being the middle mad, holding on to some good deals for others who may want to get into real estate investing or who want to find an affordable home for their budget.

Hybrid Investing

This investment is going to cross together a rental property and a flipped property. You will purchase a current rental property with the idea of adding some value to it and then reselling for a profit. You will get the benefit of getting the monthly income from the tenants while also the big payout at the end when you find a new buyer. You will need to find a property that is being offered for less than market value and rehab it to increase the value. Most of the time you will continue to rent out this property for a few years while waiting for the right timing to sell again, but you originally purchased it with the idea of selling as a flip.

Lease Options

These are more commonly known as rent to own properties. With this investment type, you will take over the funding on a property and then have the seller pay them back. Sometimes the buyer will continue to pay the "rent" for the whole duration of the lease, which will be set out in the beginning, and then once they are done, the buyer will own the home. Or the buyer will pay this rent for a year or two in order to organize their finances and get the right funding to purchase the home straight out, following the rules that they outlined with the seller in the beginning. In some cases, the investor will take the title without paying the seller's mortgage, which does cause some difficulties.

This can be beneficial because it allows the investor to make a steady income on the home for a year or two with the possibility of making a full profit at the end of that time. If the seller is not able to come up with the funding, the investor will still own the property and can choose what to do from there. This often doesn't require as much money down, but it requires a bit more legal work so you must be willing to learn about that to keep the property safe.

Tax liens

When an owner of a property doesn't pay their taxes, the local municipality is going to suffer because they still need those taxes. The tax lien will often be sold to an investor who will pay this tax and then gets the benefit of monthly interest on the property until all the amount is paid back. If the owners refuse to pay off this lien, the investor is able to foreclose on the property to get the money back.

This is not the most popular options when it comes to tax investing because it can be risky; if the owner wasn't paying the tax in the first place, why would they pay it later on. You will need to learn how to analyze a potential tax lien, be investigative, and you will not have the option of bank funding (it needs to be done in cash) so having some money available can help.

Vacation rentals

As more people are vacationing and looking for alternatives to hotels to stay in while having fun, vacation rentals have grown in popularity. Some choose to keep this small and will just rent out a home or two for families to enjoy while others are more apt to go after large rental properties that can hold a lot of people. You can choose to run these on your own, but for the bigger ones, especially if you live far away, it is best to go with a management company to help.

If you find a good rental property and offer good prices on it, this can make a great income. People are always on vacation and want somewhere comfortable in a good location to stay in. But the best properties are often in expensive areas and the previous owners may not want to bargain for a good deal with you. Take your time to search out a good location at the right price, and this can bring in a good profit.

These are some of the best strategies that you can pick to make sure you are getting the most out of your investment. It often will depend on how much work you would like to put into the project, if you want to have the income in one big chunk, if you would like to own the property while making a steady stream of income, or if you have another goal in mind. Real estate investing has options for everyone, you just need to know your goals and where you should start!

How to pick the right investing option for you

Since there are many options that come with real estate investing, many beginners wonder which option is the right one for them. In reality, there is no one option that is better than the others, but it does depend on your overall goals with your investment since each one works the best with different goals. So the first thing you need to ask is what your goals are with investing in real estate.

Picking Flipping Homes

Flipping homes can be a good option for those who want to make a lot of money in one lump sum. You will purchase a property, fix it up, and usually sell it within a few months as long as the market is doing well. In some cases, you may hold onto the home for a year or more to wait for market conditions to improve, but this will be built into your plan ahead of time.

This one goes on speed. If you take too long to fix up the home, you are losing money. Six months may not seem like a long time to fix up the home, but when you have to also consider that it can take at least a few months to sell the home and another few months before you can close. This can quickly add up in extra costs that will cut into your profits.

For people who are able to act quickly, getting all the contractors lined up and ready to go before the house even closes, and who plan out in case it takes a bit to sell the property, flipping homes can be one of the best options. It is also nice for those who aren't interested in owning the property for a long term and want to just make all the profit at once.

Picking a Renal Property

Rental properties are a unique because it provides you a steady income from month to month while allowing you to earn equity in the property all in one. If you are willing to hold onto the property, can keep tenants inside the property, and are willing to work on the maintenance and upkeep of the property, this can be the option to go with.

When purchasing property for rental purposes, you will need to be careful about the price that you get it for. You are going to have to include the mortgage, insurance, taxes, and other costs into the amount of rent and if these are too high, you will never find a tenant. Before even considering a property, you should do the math to find out if you will be able to cover the costs of keeping the property, plus make some income, while keeping the rent prices within market value.

You may need to do a bit of work on a property before you can get a tenant in. Making a few updates, adding some new paint, and changing the carpets can add a lot of value to a home without costing you too much money. You may not have to do as many updates on a rental as you would when re-selling the property, but it is still a good idea to put in a bit of work to help entice tenants to stay.

Doing background checks and having a lease can add a bit of work to the process, but ensures that you are picking good tenants to live in your apartment. The lease can help you out by listing the terms for rent prices, minimum length of stay for the tenant, and other important information.

Other options

Some beginners may prefer to use one of the other options if they are short on money to start or don't have as much time to devote to the project. Doing tax liens can give you a good start in real estate if you are short on money and want to build up.

Wholesaling in real estate can earn money without ever having to hold onto the property. Vacation rentals are good for those who want a new challenge or to open up their portfolio more, sometimes working along with other people to come up with the money, with a good return on investment.

Any of these options will help you to make money with real estate, they will just require a different type of work and amount of time that you will be in on each investment part. It is often best to start out with just one niche in the beginning to learn more about it, get your feet wet, and eventually you can expand to adding more niches into your portfolio, increasing your chances of making a large profit in the process.

Chapter 3:Financing Your Investment

Before you get too far into choosing a property and get excited about starting all the work, you need to first find the financing for the property you want. Most people will not have the money needed to purchase a home upfront when they first get started in real estate, though this is something that could occur down the line. This means that you will have to find another source of funding if you hope to make your first purchase.

Finding financing is going to be a challenge. Since there is a higher risk in real estate investing and so many people have failed in the past, many banks and other lenders have placed strict requirements on those who want to go into this choice. But learning how to work through these challenges and prepare yourself is the best way to find the financing you need to get started.

Sources for Financing

First, you need to have a good idea of where you can go to find the financing for these properties. Some of these will come to your mind right away and may be similar to what you used with a personal mortgage, such as a bank, but others will require you to get a bit more creative in the process. Some of the options that you should consider for your real estate investment include:

Banks and Financial Institutions
One of the first places that new investors will go for their funding is to a bank. If you choose this option, it is always best to go with a local bank because these have a

vested interest in seeing their communities do well and they may be more willing to help you out. While some of the requirements are stringent, if you are able to get one of these loans, you will find they are the easiest to work with and have some of the best rates.

When talking to a bank, you will notice that there are different options for you to choose from. You can see that you can choose from different interest rates, different lengths of time for the loan, and some will offer an option to forebear payments for a year or so to make it easier to concentrate on fixing and selling the property rather than on the mortgage payment.
Make sure that you take some time to talk to a banker at your local branch. They will provide you with answers to all your questions as well as an application you can fill out. This application can be lengthy, but it provides the bank with a thorough look at your financial background so they can make a better decision. Fill out everything that you can to ensure that the application is taken care of right away. Once this is complete, the banker will be able to discuss the different options that are available in your situation.

The bank is going to require you to present a lot of paperwork before handing over the money. They worry that you will be like many other real estate investors who thought they could make it, and failed so you have to prove them wrong. During this time, you may be required to have information on your debts, income, credit score, bank statements, and even letters of recommendation. A full business plan is often needed to show that you are serious and that you have thought through the steps before starting.

This does take some time and can be frustrating to a new investor. But banks are often one of the best choices in terms of rates and options compared to anyone else. You should build up a good relationship with them, even if you end up using one of the other funding sources. You never know when you may need the bank for another project later on.

Look for local investors
With a little bit of networking and research, you may find that there are investors in your area who want to get into the real estate market, or diversify their portfolio, but they just don't have the time to do all the work on their own. These individuals may be willing to "hire" you to do the work by lending you the money to get started. This can be a great way to fund the whole project, or at least get a bit of extra help along the way.

Even when working with a local investor you will need to be prepared. They are not going to just hand over their money to someone who makes big promises without any proof. Bring along a business plan and other information that the investor may need to make a decision. You and the investor should also create a contract concerning how long you get to pay the money back and the amount that the investor will earn extra for helping you out.

Family and friends
Another avenue that you may want to consider when starting your real estate business is to ask friends and family. This is often the best rates since those close to you may be willing to loan the money for nothing back, or a much lower price than the banks and investors, and they often don't want to look at your finances or your credit score. Keep in mind that loaning money can bring

about some hurt feelings if everyone isn't on the same page. Just like with any financial transaction, write up a contract with terms that both parties can agree to in order to keep everyone happy.

Crowdsourcing

For those who are handy with using social media and spreading out the word, crowdsourcing can be a great option. This gives you a chance to ask others to help with the investment. You do need to be a bit creative here as there are thousands of others asking for help as well and you want to stand out from the crowd. Consider writing out a great post, sharing the information with as many people as possible, and even offer an incentive to everyone who contributes.

Use your own money

The best way to get the property of your choice is to use your own money. This allows you to not have to worry about paying anyone back and there is no mortgage or interest to pay each month. You can avoid contracts, hurt feelings, interest rates, ad other issues when you just bring your own money to the table.

The biggest issue with this one is that most people do not have the full price of a house or another property just lying around. But even a little bit can make a big difference. Banks and other investors look much more favorably on those who are able to come up with a sizeable down payment for their investment compared to those who come in and have nothing saved up. Having some of your own money to put towards the project, even if it isn't much, will help you out when looking for funding.

Getting the funding you need

Getting the right funding for your real estate investment is no easy task. Many banks and investors are wary of helping someone out who has no experience and they want to be reassured that you are going to be the best person for the job. There are a few things that you can do that will help you succeed with getting your funding, no matter which choice you go with. Some of the steps that you should take include:

- Come up with a down payment—any amount is going to help, but the larger the down payment, the more likely that the banks and other lenders will cover the rest.

- Bolster up your financial history—this can take some time so get started early. Try to get your credit score up as high as possible, with 740 or above being the best. Make sure that you are watching your debts and paying off as many of them as possible, clearing off bad stuff on the credit report, and paying everything on time. A good mix of account is good as well, though you shouldn't try opening new accounts right before applying for a property loan.

- Avoid the bigger banks—these often have no vested interest in you and will turn you away for little things. You are just a number to them and it really
- doesn't matter to them if you get the money or not. But with a small local bank, you are able to meet with the people, become a face and a name, and they have an interest in helping their community thrive so they are more likely to give you the money.
- Complete the full application—yes the application is long and you would rather do something else, but make sure that you fill it all out before submitted. Also, any time the bank asks for some more information, get it to them quickly to expedite the process.

Getting started in real estate can take some time and some patience, but if you are willing to put in the work, and can find the right financing in the process, you will find that it can be one of the most varied and wonderful investment types.

Chapter 4: Finding Your First Property and Making a Profit

The next thing to work on in real estate investing is finding the property you want to purchase. This is often one of the most exciting times in the adventure because you can begin the search. All the possibilities seem endless and you are ready to get out there and see which property will be yours. And of course, thinking about the profit can be a good incentive during this stage as well.

As a beginner, you should not just jump into the process without doing a bit of research as well. Understanding what your shopping criteria are, finding the right area to purchase, and getting the property purchased are all big steps to take.

Shopping Criteria

Before going out and looking at houses, you need to make a list of shopping criteria. It is easy to get out there and fall in love with a house and throw caution to the wind. This sometimes works out, but if you don't stay with your plans, you will often end up with a property that doesn't meet your goals and you may be stuck with it for some time.

There are a few things that you may look at when picking out your first property. You will want to look at the location, the price, how much work you will need to put into the home, and if the property will work for your needs. Other things that you should consider and have on your selection criteria list include:

- Property size
- Property conditions
- Lot size
- Number of units when renting
- Cash flow
- Cap rate
- Appreciation potential
- Neighborhood and town

Write out this list before ever going to look at a property and keep it close by. Any time you want to purchase a property, you should take a look at the list and make sure it fits your criteria. While there are some instances when you can deviate from the selection criteria, this is the best way to keep your eyes on the prize.

Price

A good place to start is to look at the price of the home. You need to determine how much you can really make off a home and still keep it within market value. For example, if you are looking at a home that is being sold for $150,00 and the market around that house goes between $140,000 and $155,000, it may not be the best deal for you.

First, you most likely won't be able to sell the home above that $155,000 mark unless there is a big turn coming in the market. Second, any repairs and updates you do will probably cost you more than $5000 on the home to make it worth your time. Add in closing costs, mortgage payments, insurance, and other costs you will incur while owning the property, and you will probably not make anything.

Now, let's look at that same house for $150,000. But you find this house in a neighborhood or market that typically has homes worth $200,000 or more. If you can do some simple updates and keep your costs lower, you will make a good profit and have a fairly easy time selling the home.

This is why it's so important to do your market research before starting. If you didn't research first, you may have purchased the house in the first example and lost out on any profit.

You need to use these same ideas when renting out a property. You can't purchase a home that is too expensive for the neighborhood and expect someone to rent it out at enough to cover costs. When purchasing a rental property, you need to remember that the costs of mortgage, insurance, taxes, and so on need to be covered in the rent that the tenant pays you. If you figure up your costs and the rent comes out above market value or rent prices in that area, it is best to find a different property.

Where to look for your property

Even in a down economy, there are always properties for sale. Not all of them are going to meet your criteria, but there is always something. The trick for the real estate investor is to look in many different locations to find the best deals, hopefully before someone else snatches them up. Some of the places where you should look to find the perfect property include:

MLS

The Multiple Listing Service is a great place to get started. If the property is listed with a real estate agent, any of them, in the area, the MLS will show it. You can look at properties throughout the country, although it is usually best to just look at which properties are for sale in your chosen area. Most of the listing are with agents, but there are some for sale by owners that will pop up too. Realtor.com and Redfin.com are good examples of finding homes on the MLS.

Newspaper

While newspaper is not always going to have a comprehensive list of properties available, there are sometimes a few gems that pop up. For sale by owners like to use the newspaper as an efficient way to get the news out. Often the homes in the newspaper will be for a good discount so they are worth your time to check out.

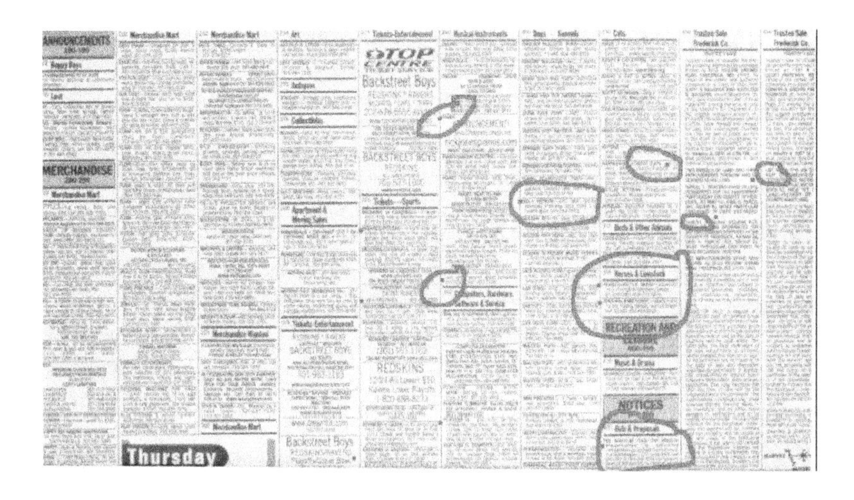

Word of mouth

When you get into real estate investing, you will need to get the hang of networking. Some of your best deals will be found through word of mouth. You may hear from a friend that someone lost their job or needs to move quickly and is willing to sell a home for quickly. Maybe someone alerts you to a new development coming into town and you decide to purchase discounted property there before it goes up. There are many ways that your network of friends and acquaintances will be able to help you so get started with meeting new people and growing your business.

Craigslist

While you should always use caution when using craigslist to make sure you are dealing with real people and won't get scammed (never send money for a property online), craigslist is a great place to start to find a good deal. Many people who are selling their own homes, and even some agents, will use craigslist because it will hit a large amount of people and posting is free. It can at least help you find some leads that could bring in the profits. Usually checking every few days or once a week can help you out.

Outbound Marketing

Sometimes, you need to let the seller come to you. Putting some advertising in the newspaper or other sources can alert potential sellers that you are in the market for their home. When a seller needs to sell quickly or can offer you a good deal on the home, they can see your advertising and can come to you. While most of your properties will come from actively searching for the property, you may be able to get a few good leads this way.

Finding the property

With your search criteria, you should be able to find the right property that will meet your needs. You can go out with a real estate agent to look at homes or talk to the owners themselves if you are more interested in a for sale by owner property. Every time you look at a home, take your search criteria with you and figure out if it is going to work for your needs.

Now, there are some times when you may need to go off the search criteria to get the perfect property. If the property meets most of your standards but is off on just one little thing, it could still be a good investment. The search criteria are not meant to keep you from good deals, but they should be used as a way to prevent impulse buying that can get you in trouble.

Before you put an offer in on a property, make sure to start gathering a few numbers. Figure out what you will want to fix or update in the home and then go talk to a few contractors to find out the cost of materials and work, even if you choose to do it on your own. You will need to figure this into the final cost of the home to find out if it is worth your time.

Making a deal on the property

With your search criteria in hand and some time looking through the market, you have finally found the property you want to purchase. As this time, you may want to consider bringing a realtor on board to help you out. While it is possible to do these sales on your own and may save you some money, as a beginner it is nice to have someone who knows the ropes helping you out.

Now it is time to put in an offer on the property you would like to purchase. Be ready for some negotiation. You will most likely put in an offer below what the seller asks for and they are going to bargain with you to see how high you'll go. Hopefully both parties can come to a number they are happy with and the sale goes through!

Once the seller does accept your offer, there is still more work to be done. If you funded this project through a bank, they will require you to get inspections done on the home to make sure it is safe, as well as an appraisal to see how much the home is worth in case you don't succeed. These inspections can be beneficial to you as well because they give you a good idea of what needs to be fixed up around the home, can put some of the work on the buyers to fix the property, and can give you an out if something major is wrong with the property.

This process can take a bit of time depending on the inspections and how much needs to be fixed up before the bank will give you financing. But by preparing ahead of time, you can speed up the process and get to work with creating your new profit. Keep in mind that once the papers are signed and the keys handed over, the click starts ticking for you to get the work done.

Making your property profitable

Once all the paperwork is signed and you have the keys in hand, the clock is going to start ticking. You get a bit of time before the first mortgage is due, but you have a lot to get done in that time. You need to come up with a plan to fix up the property to sell it or start renting it out before too much time goes by, or you start to see a dip in your profits.

The first thing to do is go through the property and make all necessary changes. If you were lucky, the property won't need much in changes; it was just sold so low due to economic downturns and other issues. But with many properties, you will need to put in the legwork to get it looking nice and up to the price where you can profit.

Once the home looks nice, you have two decisions. You can decide to rent out the property to others or you can put it back on the market to sell. Renting can be nice if you would like to have a steady income and grow equity, but remember that the rent needs to pay your mortgage and other costs, even when a tenant is not in the building. When picking a tenant, do a background check to make sure they pay their bills and got along with their past tenants. The background check may cost a few dollars, but it helps ensure that you get good tenants who won't destroy the building, who will pay on time, and who will stick around in the property for longer.

For those who don't want to deal with the property every month and would rather get the one-time profit, flipping homes can be a great option. With this one, you will really need to move quickly because not only do you need time to make the necessary adjustments to the home, but you also need at least a few months to have the home for sale before someone makes a purchase. The longer you hold onto the property, either while making repairs or while waiting for it to sell, the more money it will cost you.

Hopefully you are able to make the changes and sell the property quickly, but plan for it to take a little bit of time. Once you sell your property, you can use some of that money to roll into another investment property and start it all over again. Soon you can purchase two or three properties and even go into another niche, such as flipping some of the homes and renting out others, to really increase your portfolio. As you learn the ropes, it will be easier to take on more properties and funding can come a bit faster as you build up a relationship with your banker.

Chapter 5: Working with Others Can Make Things Easier

Many beginners in real estate investing feel that they have to do things all on their own. But those who are successful in real estate investing are the ones who know that it takes a whole team to make this work. Through every step of this process, you will have to work along with others who can help you find the properties, fix them up, provide funding, and even sell the home when you're done. Setting up this team right from the beginning can make things easier and will ensure your success.

Real Estate Agents

One of the first people you should add to your network is a real estate agent or two. You will be amazed at the amount of knowledge that a real estate agent will be able to provide you. They know the area really well and have been watching the market trends for a long time. They know how much properties are worth in different parts of town and can discuss whether they will go up or down with you in the near future. They know if someone is considering selling their home soon or not. They know the laws pertaining to the real estate market and can help you place a bid on a new property and fill out all the paperwork.

Even after you purchase a new property, you can still use a real estate agent. They can help you to list your home, offering the biggest range of views compared to just doing it yourself, helping you to sell it quickly. Over time, you can build up a great relationship with a real estate agent. This person can help you find new properties, purchase them, and re-sell them later on.

There are quite a few agents you can choose to work in depending on the area you want to work. Sit down and talk to a few different agents and see who has experience with your investment type and who will be able to propel your business forward.

Contractors

There are two ways you can go about fixing up the property that you purchase. Some decide that they will do all the work themselves. This is going to take up more of your free time, but when you don't have to pay for labor and hours worked from a contractor, it can save you a lot of money. For those who know how to do a lot of the work in their homes and are willing to put in the time and effort, doing the work yourself makes sense.

But many people decide to hire a contractor to do the work. It may cost them a little bit more, but a contractor can often do a better job than most individuals and they are much faster, saving time that the property is sitting unused. Finding good contractors can take some time, so start looking earlier. You can choose to go with a general contractor who will be able to take on most of the projects for your property, or you can find individuals to work on different projects as you need.

Any time that you meet a new contractor, especially one who is able to do something unique for a property, get their business information and store it. This will help you out if one of your other contractors isn't available or you need something new done in your property.

Accountants

Unless you are really good at organizing your information and can keep accurate records the whole time, you may want to consider hiring an accountant. They can help you to keep track of your real estate finances and will alert you to how much money has been spent, how much you will need to sell the property for to make money and so much more. If you aren't good at dealing with numbers or don't have the time to keep track of all the finances of your project, working with an accountant is the best option.

When tax season comes around, you will find that your accountant will be your best friend. Tax season can be hard for those working in real estate because the rules are always changing. Your accountant can look over your information and determine how much you earned for the year and what you are able to claim as deductions to save even more money. Some investors worry that an accountant will cost them too much money, but the amount they can save you during tax time makes it worth it.

Mentors

In any business, it is a good idea to have a mentor who will be able to help you along the way. No matter how much you research your chosen business, there are going to be times when you have questions, when things may be tougher than you imagined, or that another issue comes up. With a mentor, you will have someone you can call when times get tough and who can give you motivation to continue on.

A mentor can come in many forms. Some people work with others in the industry, those who have been investing in real estate, to learn the trade. They may work part time by helping out with flipping a home or they will work in property management for someone who already rents out properties. This allows them to have some hands on experience in the industry and are more prepared to take on the challenges that comes with real estate investing.

If you are not able to work under someone else, you can still find a mentor to help you out. Real estate agents are a good choice because they have a lot of experience in these matters and can tell you who is selling, where to look for good deals, and even information on the best ways to improve a home. Finding someone who works in rental properties or flipping homes who is willing to answer your questions and help you out. Even working with someone in business, even those that aren't directly related to real estate can help you out.

Bankers

Unless you already have a lot of money in savings and can purchase a whole property without any help, you will need a bank or other funding source to give you the money to get started. If you plan to stay in real estate for some time, you will need to get a good relationship with the banker because you will spend a lot of time talking with them and getting more funding for each proceeding project.

Finding a good banker is critical. You need to have someone who will be on your side, someone who can answer your questions and be there when you need assistance, and someone who is interested in helping you through the whole process. Local bankers are often the best to work with for this because they will put a name with the face and will really work to help you out.

You need a good relationship with your banker if you want things to get done quickly. It may take a bit of time in the beginning to get the financing in order, but if you work well with your banker and continue to use them for your future projects, the process becomes more streamlined and the funding can become faster each time.

Others in your network

When you get into real estate, you should start networking as early as possible. Even before getting your funding or looking for the first property, you need to get out there and find people who can be a part of your network. Knowing someone who works at the bank, who may be selling their home down the road, who can do deck work or fix up a basement, and more can help you out in the future.

Any new connection is important. While it may seem like a friendship now or you may not need to utilize the connection right away, you never know when it may come in handy later. For example, you can meet someone new at a church event and then a year or two down the line, they offer to sell you their home for a great discount or they will need to purchase a new home and you can offer your project to them.

Make new network connections wherever you go. There is never a bad time for networking in the real estate business. Any time you go out, to the grocery store, to church, to a school event, and everywhere else, you can meet someone new and grow your business.

To start your real estate business, you need to be ready to take on some new challenges, find the best properties for a good price, and to make the best choices to increase the value of the property. And with the right team and the right connections, it becomes easier than ever to see all your hard work in real estate turn to profit.

Chapter 6: Easy Ways to Increase the Value of Your Property without Spending Too Much.

Once you own the new property, it is important to get started on the fixes right away. Whether you are selling the property as soon as possible or want to rent it out, there are usually little fixes you will have to make that will increase the value of your home without costing too much.

There are always a million things that you could fix in a new home, but if you are trying to flip the house, you don't want to waste time on things that are not that important or won't provide a good return on investment. For example, painting the walls in the home is an inexpensive way to brighten up the house and can increase the overall value. But doing a complete upgrade on the kitchen or the bathroom will just be a waste of money in these situations. Learning the simple fixes you can do to increase the value of a home will make all the difference, especially if you're in a hurry.

Some of the things that you can do that won't cost a lot of money but which will increase the value of a home include:

- Cleaning—one of the first things that you should do when taking ownership of a new property is perform a deep cleaning. This means both the inside and the outside of the property. Get rid of garbage, clean the carpets and the walls, make sure that all odors are gone, and make the home feel more pleasant.

- Paint—there is nothing as simple as paint for increasing the value of a home. A fresh coat of paint, changed to a modern or neutral tone, will really draw the customers in and make it easier to sell the home. Plus paint is not going to cost a lot of money and can be done in a few days.

- Add some curb appeal—take a look outside the house and determine what you can do to encourage buyers to come in the door. Adding a new mailbox, putting in a few plants, or repainting the window trim and shutters are all simple fixes that will make the home look more inviting. You should also maintain the nice plants that are already there and keep the grass mowed and walkways clear.

- Change some fixtures—fixture usually don't cost a lot of money, but will be important when it comes to selling the home. if a cabinet handle, light fixture, light switch cover, or even doorknob are broken or out dated, spending a few dollars to update these could help to sell the home faster.

- Add in more light—if the property has lots of windows, draw back the sashes and let it come right in. Rooms that look light and airy do so well when being shown off to potential buyers. If your property is low on windows, you should add in a few more lamps and make sure that the lightbulbs are all working properly to help add in some of that light.

- Stage the property—sometimes the way that the property is staged will help to determine if you are going to be able to sell it or not. And if the property doesn't have any furniture, it can hinder the progress even more. Bring in some furniture (you could get a set that you use at each home you flip) and stage it around the home to make it look more inviting and appealing to potential buyers.
- Change the flooring—this one can get a bit more expensive if you aren't careful about your choices, but many potential buyers like to see that the carpet is fresh and well taken care of. If you purchase a property with old, faded, and frayed carpet, it is best to get it replaced. Even a cheap remnant carpet will help to change the look and feel of the home. If the carpet is in pretty good shape still, make sure that it gets a good cleaning before showing.

Updates that aren't worth the cost

Updates are one place where you need to be careful. There are so many things that you can do with a home, but there are some updates that are really expensive and won't bring hardly any value to your home. Some of the updates that you should avoid when flipping the home include:

Adding in a pool

Pools can be tricky when it comes to adding in value to the home. If the home is in a warmer climate, it may help out a bit and draw the potential buyers in, but anywhere that has colder months, it will not be worth your time. No matter where you live though, you probably won't get all of the money back that you spent on the pool. Pools are expensive to put in and while it may bring in a few more buyers, they often aren't willing to put enough extra money to pay for the pool.

Not only will you have the issues of not getting the money back from a pool, but some buyers are turned off by homes that have pools. Buyers with small children, those who want a yard that is low maintenance, and those who don't have a big budget for taking care of the pool will turn away from homes that have pools, making it harder to sell the home.

Too much customization

Customizations can really harm the resell value of your home. Most homebuyers will want to make their own customizations and while you can spend thousands on that kitchen, the yardwork, and other detailed customizations, you will find that the buyer won't really care about these since they plan to make their own changes.

Sometimes these customizations are going to cost you. You can spend a lot of money on something you like, but if your buyer is thinking about much it will cost them to make updates, they may be less willing to purchase the home or will offer a lower price. When choosing customizations, keep things simple, find inexpensive methods to update that still look nice, and you will get your money back.

Room conversions

You need to be really careful when it comes to converting rooms. Most potential buyers will have a checklist that they want to fill out when purchasing a home and if you can meet with this check list, you are more likely to sell the home. Getting rid of spaces, especially bedrooms, can really cost you when it comes to selling the home. You may think that getting rid of a room for a walk-in closet is the best idea, but this can cost a lot ad most buyers would rather have that extra room.

For the most part, leave the rooms how they originally are in the home. Changing them can be expensive and since most potential buyers are going to have their own ideas of how they want the house to be, they will probably make changes anyway. Unless you can find a simple and inexpensive way to add in another good sized room to the home, other room conversions are not worth your time.

Small gains in square footage

Adding square footage can go two ways. If you are able to update a basement for little money and make it livable, you can increase the value of the home with all this extra space. But smaller additions of square footage could end up harming your home value. For example, adding in a sunroom may seem like a great idea, but it is usually a huge undertaking and most buyers aren't going to see it as adding value to the home.

There are many small changes you can make to the square footage that won't increase the value. For example, adding in space that doesn't match well with the layout of the home will decrease the value and putting new rooms in weird places, such as a new bathroom that requires walking through the kitchen to get to, may not offer a good return on investment.

Over improving

When making adjustments to the new property, you need to take into account the neighborhood. You do not want to make the home too different from the rest of the neighborhood, or you will not get the full value. You will find that your neighborhood is going to greatly influence the price of your home so any improvements that you make on the home should fit in with the neighborhood, or it is not worth your neighborhood.

If you are uncertain about what is common in your neighborhood, you should tour some open houses in the area. You can see what income level the neighborhood is at and then make adjustments to ensure that you are making improvements that will fit in with the neighborhood but won't turn away the right potential buyers.

Kitchens and bathrooms

While a new kitchen or a bathroom can look really nice in the home, you are not going to get all the money back from this investment. Completely remodeling the bathroom and kitchen can cost a lot of money and while they will draw in some more potential buyers than a run down looking kitchen and bathroom, you will find that it doesn't increase the value as much as you hoped.

This does not mean you can't go through and make some minor changes to these areas to make them look better. First, the kitchen. If you have an older style kitchen with carpet, consider finding some inexpensive laminate to update the flooring and make it look nicer. Replace the fixtures such as cabinet knobs and faucet and add in a backsplash to change up the look. Updating a few appliances can help and a fresh coat of paint makes all the difference.

For the bathroom, you will need to be careful with the updates you make. Changing everything will just take too much time and money from the overall project. But adding in some new lights, changing the handles on the bathroom cupboards, and replace the toilet seat. These can help to brighten up the bathroom and give it a new look with only a few dollars spent.

Doing updates on a home can really help to increase the value of the home and make it more appealing to potential homebuyers, but you have to be careful about which updates you choose. Some may look really nice, but if they cost more than you will get out of the home, they aren't worth your time. Avoid some of the costly updates listed above and stick with simple fixes that don't cost a lot and are easy to get done in a short amount of time.

Chapter 7: Tips Every Real Estate Investing Beginner Should Know

Getting into real estate is challenging. You want to make a great profit, but finding a home that is a good deal, that won't take up all your time and money to fix, and will sell for a great price is going to take some time. Too many people fail in this business because they aren't able to keep up with the work or they jump in without doing their research. If you are considering getting started in real estate, here are a few tips you should follow to get yourself on the right path to success.

- Treat it like a business—this is not a get rich quick scheme, this is actual work. If you go into real estate thinking that you can do a bit of work whenever you want and it is going to sell for thousands of dollars in profit in just a few weeks, you are going to be hurting pretty quickly. To see success in real estate, you need to treat this just like you would any other business. Have goals in mind for the next two, five, and even ten years and consider writing up a business plan to keep everything together.

- Check out your credit—any time you want to get some funding, you are going to have banks and other lending sources looking at your credit score. The higher you can get this score, at least 700, the better rates and terms you will get on your mortgage. Check that your credit is looking good, pay all your bills on time, and find ways to lower your debt to income ratio if possible before applying for any kind of funding.

- Find a good mortgage broker—not all banks or brokers are the same. You could talk to ten different banks and they will offer you various interest rates and terms. It is a good idea to shop around a little bit. This allows you to see what is out there and to determine who will give you the best deals on your funding. Also, consider going with a local bank. They usually have deals that the bigger ones will leave out and they are easier to work with.

- Be picky when looking at areas—there may be some areas near you that have great neighborhoods and good prices, but how are they going to do in the future? There may be a great acreage right out of town, but if it is hours from the nearest town, how much will you actually be able to sell it for? All of these questions and more are important when determining where you would like to purchase a home.

- Network—there is nothing more important than networking with others who are in the industry. Find other investors who have been in the market for some time and who would be willing to answer some of your questions. Talk to real estate agents and find out which properties may be coming for sale. Go to business events and get involved in your local community to meet as many people as possible. You never know when you will need one of these connections to make real estate investing easier. While you are at it, consider joining a local real estate club to learn more about the trends of the industry.

- Look around for properties—too many new investors spend their time looking just on the MLS. They think this is the only way they can find properties to purchase and sell. But some of the best deals are found in other ways, such as auction sites, in the newspaper, or word of mouth. While the MLS is a place to start, you should consider expanding out to look at multiple sources to find the perfect property.

- Read up on real estate—as with any business you deal with, you need to educate yourself. Purchasing a real estate book or subscribing to a few different magazines in the industry can help you to learn more about investing and can keep you up to date on the current trends in the market. Simple shifts in interest rates, new buildings coming into the area, government regulations and more can influence how the real estate market will go and when you read up on current events, you are better prepared to rework your business to benefit from these changes.

- Work with a realtor—while it is possible to do this process on your own and it could save some money, working with a realtor can help out immensely. Realtors know the business and can point you towards a good property to purchase, help you put in an offer, fill out all the paperwork, and help you again when it's time to sell the home. Realtors also know the area and can be a good source of information when you start this journey.

- Don't get too excited—it is not a good idea to get too excited about a home before you do your research. A lot of things can happen during the purchasing of a home and you don't want to get too attached or feel disappointed because it fell through. You may find that the home doesn't meat your search criteria, someone else outbids you, or something else goes wrong. Keeping a cool head can make it easier to move on from a property if something doesn't work out.

- Never get attached to the property—since you will not be living in the home or using it for personal use, it doesn't do any good to get attached to a property. First off, getting attached in the early parts of purchasing the property can make it disappointing if something falls through and you don't even obtain the property. Then if you become attached to the property while fixing it up, it is hard to take a critical eye to the property to fix it up or you may not think reasonably about selling it. Always think about this as a business or a project you are working on, not something of personal value.

- Find a mentor to help—getting into the real estate industry can be tough. There are many variances in the market, finding a property can take time, and often it is hard to understand how much work is really involved until you are in the middle of it. Finding a mentor can really make a difference while providing you with the extra motivation you need at times. Some of the most successful people in real estate choose to work under someone else, working as an assistant for some time so they can learn about real estate before starting. Even if you can't find someone to work under, finding someone with experience who can answer your questions and gives advice can be invaluable.

- Keep good records—you need to keep good records of everything you are doing in real estate. This is going to be used to help determine how much you earned on the process, important during tax time, and can influence how much you can deduct to save money. Hire an accountant or get a good program to help keep all your real estate finances in order.

- Keep all receipts—it is going to be hard to convince your tax accountant to give you the deductions you want at the end of the year if you have no way to prove that you spent the money. Everything that you do should be recorded and keep them in a safe place to help you save money.

- Pick the right updates—any updates that you do to the property will start to cost you, but there are some that will greatly increase the value of the property and others that won't help you get your money back. Learning which ones are the most beneficial to your project will help you to make as much money as possible on this endeavor.

Getting started in real estate can be a big undertaking. You may be excited about making some money on the side or replace your full time income, but there is a lot of risk with real estate and it can take up a lot of your time and energy. Following these simple tips will help you get prepared for starting your own business and seeing success in the real estate market.

Conclusion

Thank you again for purchasing this book!
I hope this book was able to help you to understand real estate investing and how it can be a great way to increase your income, either part time or full time, and put your money to work for you.

The next step is to decide if real estate investing is the right choice for you. While it is possible to make some good money with real estate investing, it is not the right choice for everyone. For those who are ready to get their hands dirty, learn more about the market around them, and want to really see their income grow, you then need to determine what type of real estate you would like to invest in.

This guidebook will help you to determine if real estate investing is right for you, help you to get the proper funding, where to look for properties, and the team you need to ensure you are getting the most out of your investment. With a little research and hard work, you will find that investing in real estate can be a rewarding choice.

Finally, if you enjoyed this book, please take the time to share your thoughts and post a review. It'd be greatly appreciated!

Thank you and good luck!

Sales Page

Getting into real estate can be one of the most rewarding experiences of your life. You get to choose your own hours, the properties you want to use, and even the niche that will best suit your needs within the market. For those who like to put in some work to see their money grow, real estate investing is one of the best options out there.

This guidebook is going to spend some time talking about real estate investing and how you will be able to make this work to see your income grow. Whether you are interested in wholesaling homes, flipping homes, or using them as rental properties, you will find all the answers that you need and more inside this guidebook.

- There is so much that you can learn about real estate investing include:
- What is real estate investing
- The best strategies to make your money grow
- How to find the perfect strategy
- Who you need to have on your team for success
- Selling the property
- Property updates that increase the value
- And more

When you are ready to start putting your money to work and seeing where your income can go, make sure to check out this guidebook and see what real estate investing can do for you.

Part 2 - Real Estate Flipping

How to Flip Houses for Passive Income

By Sabi Shepherd

Additionally, the information in the following pages is intended only for informational purposes and should thus be thought of as universal. As befitting its nature, it is presented without assurance regarding its prolonged validity or interim quality. Trademarks that are mentioned are done without written consent and can in no way be considered an endorsement from the trademark holder.

Introduction

Congratulations on purchasing this book and thank you for doing so.

The following chapters will focus on real estate investing and discuss more ways that you can make a profit from flipping houses. Be sure to check out Volume 1 before you dive into this book for many of the basic fundamentals that this book will by its very nature be expanding upon.

There are plenty of books on this subject on the market, thanks again for choosing this one! Every effort was made to ensure it is full of as much useful information as possible, please enjoy!

Chapter 1: How to Get Financing for Deals

One of the biggest hurdles that investors will have to jump is getting financing for the deals that they have found. Without financing, they are unable to buy the home or the property and they haven't really found a deal at all. Finding the right investing is key to being able to make money on property.

Good Rates

The first thing that you should look for when you are financing an investment property is great rates. The rates should be relatively low and should be able to help you avoid paying a lot just to own the property. A good rule of thumb for a real estate investment property mortgage would be to keep the interest rate at or below 4%.

Getting a good rate will do two things for you: it will save you extra money on the mortgage that you are paying while you are flipping the property and it will enable you to free up money for your expenses.

In order to get a mortgage rate that is as low as possible, you should make sure that your credit is in great standing and that you have the cash for the down payment. While these things are very helpful when you are trying to get a low mortgage rate, they are not necessarily the only thing that you will need to have. You may also be able to get the financing for your investment property without either of these things – more on this later!

Short Terms

When you are applying for the mortgage, it is important to let your lender know that you plan to only have the property for a short time before you attempt to sell it for a profit. This can change things in the way of what you will be paying for a mortgage.

A 30-year mortgage is a great option if you want to make your payments lower while you are flipping the house. It may be harder, though, to sell the home if you have a 30-year on it.

While you will pay more on a monthly basis while you are flipping, a 15-year may be the best way to go for your home. It will be much easier, and you will have more wiggle room if you get a 15-year mortgage on the investment property. Even if you are unable to sell the house right away, you will likely be able to rent it out.

Depending on your lender, you may be able to get a short-term mortgage. These come with different options, and the newest ones cater to people just like you: flippers. They are intended for people who do not plan to keep the house for themselves and who do not want to be tethered to a decades-long mortgage.

No Cash

The easiest way to get a home without any cash would be to get a 100% mortgage. This is only for people who have excellent credit or who have been in the military. Not all lenders offer this option. Check with your lender to see if your down payment can be included in the mortgage.

If you have another home, you can get an HELOC loan to finance the down payment. The Home Equity Line of Credit will allow you to borrow against your other property and you can use that to pay for the down payment. If you are just getting started with flipping, you can use your own home but understand that you will still be responsible for the payment even if your flip is a flop.

Another option for people with very good credit is to get a credit card that you can charge the down payment on. As long as you have a high limit, you should have no problem doing this on the end of your credit card. Be sure to check with your lender before you secure the credit line, some lenders do not allow this.

People who have poor credit can still get a house with no cash in hand, but they will have to get a little bit creative with it. As long as you own something that people may want, you could consider trading them the item for the down payment. This works if you have a vehicle or land that you are willing to get rid of. It's usually only works for homes that are for sale by the owner.

Poor Credit

What happens if you have the cash that you need for a down payment, but you have poor credit? There are a few things that you can do.

The first thing that you should consider doing is getting a really inexpensive property. In some areas, you can find a house for around the same as what you would pay in a down payment in other areas. The house will probably be in very poor condition, but it will give you a chance to truly flip it. You can then sell it for a profit and repeat the process moving onto larger (and more expensive) houses. This method does not require you to get any type of mortgage.

Your next option would be to consider an FHA loan. These are only available to first time home buyers so make sure that you are really ready to do this. Live in the house while you are flipping it so that you are truly using it as your first purchased home. You can get an FHA loan with a score as low as 500, but be prepared to pay around 10% for a down payment.

Seller financing has become so popular in the past 5 years. This is due to the fact that people just don't have the credit scores required to get a good mortgage or a mortgage at all. With seller financing, the seller will allow you to purchase the house and make a payment on it. The only difference in this is that the lender is the actual seller of the house and not a bank that you would typically pay your payment to. You can save some money by doing this but you may not get all of the guarantees that you would with a bank.

Unconventional

There are many unconventional methods that you can use to find financing for an investment property if you do not have the cash or credit score that you would typically need for one of these homes. Hard lenders and partnerships are the most common ways for investors to get started with flipping properties.

Hard lenders are people or businesses who have a lot of money to spare and want to make some extra on top of that. They will loan the money to you in the same way that a mortgage company would. The interest rate may be very high, though, because that is how they make the money back and earn money off of it. This is one option that you should consider as a last resort because of the high interest rates. Many hard lenders offer terms that are much shorter than traditional mortgages, around 3 years is the maximum amount of time that most offer.

A very popular southern California couple started their extremely successful flipping business with the help of a partner, and you can start yours the same way. A partner is someone who you likely know from personal or business connections. The partner has the money to finance the deal while you have the skills to flip the property. Each partner that you work with will have different terms but the most common is the partner fully financing the flip and taking a 50/50 split of the profits from it. This option is great if you truly have no money, no credit and no place to start with your flip.

Chapter 2: Good Investment Properties

The amount that you stand to make is largely dependent on the type of property that you choose to invest in. Investing in a really great property can (and will) allow you the opportunity to make a lot of money. While investing in a property that isn't quite right for you will cause you to lose a lot of money. Finding a great investment property shouldn't be hard and looking at some of these types will be able to help you with the finding the one that is perfect for you.

Decent Properties

Even if you want to truly flip the property, you should consider a property that is in decent shape. While you may not want a home that is brand new or recently renovated, the less money you have to pour into the home, the better. It will save you money and will increase the profit margin on the property.

The mistake that a lot of first time flippers make is finding a property that is in terrible shape. These properties often have hidden problems that the buyers do not see when they first purchase it. Buying a property that is in really poor shape can cause you to lose money and may make your situation worse than when you first started.

If you buy a property that is in decent shape, you will likely only need to make cosmetic changes to it to be able to sell it for a profit. You may pay more for the property when you first purchase it and this could seem like a problem but you will be able to save more money on the property during the flip. You could then sell it at a higher profit which would pay off in the end.

When you are looking for homes, consider looking at ones that are not brand new but are also not completely dilapidated. Save the big mess properties for later on when you have the budget to incur the high costs that come with unexpected problems in the home that you have purchased and are flipping.

High-Buy Areas

It may be really tempting to buy a property and flip it in an area where the housing prices are much higher than the average, but this may not be your best option. It is especially important when you are first getting started with your business that you find homes that are in high cash flow areas as opposed to places that have high prices. You must make sure that you are going to be able to sell the house that you plan on flipping.

While a beach property may seem like the best option for you, save this one for later on in your flipping career. Try to find a home that is in a median area or one that has homes that fall in the average price range. While these homes may not be showstoppers, they are the ones that are going to sell.

High cash flow areas will allow you to make a higher profit margin on the property that you have flipped and have a quicker sale on it. If you think about it, it really makes sense. There are many more people who are looking for an average home in a suburban area than there are people who are looking for an extravagant second home on the beach.

Non-Investment Properties

Wait...you wanted an investment property, though, right? Yes, that is exactly what you want but don't go for a property that someone has already invested in.

Whether you are planning to flip and sell at a profit or flip and rent out to high-credit tenants, you need to make sure that you have a great home for the people who are going to be living in the house next. This starts with making sure that you don't buy someone else's investment property.

If you are truly serious about flipping the property, it is important that there are not tenants there left over from the previous owner who used it for rental passive income. It can take months to get the current tenants out of the home so you can start your flip. Even when you do manage to get them out in a timely fashion, it is hard to tell the damage that they will do to the property out of spite for having to leave the home that they have been living in. It is always better when you don't have to deal with any type of tenants in an investment situation.

Note: if you are not planning on flipping the property and simply want passive income from a tenant, be sure to *look* for properties that already have a tenant in them which can save you a lot of headaches in the process of renting it out.

Newer Market Properties

Always look for houses that have just come on the market. There may be a lot more competition with these types of homes, but you will be able to get a home that is a better deal, and that has not sat on the market for a long time. If you are quick and offer the right amount, you will probably get the house before other investors even have a chance to check the home out.

The biggest problem with houses that have been on the market for a long time is that there is a reason that they have been on the market. They may have major problems with the guts of the home, or they may have problems cosmetically. If they are not selling, they may even be in an area that does not have a high cash flow. If the property has been on the market for months or years, the chances are that you will have a hard time selling it once you purchase it and flip it. You may even have a hard time renting it out if the area is bad enough.

A secondary problem that can come from homes that have sat for a long time is vandalism. Criminals take note of homes that do not have any residents, and they use them. They could be using them to live in, they could have destroyed them for fun, or they could even be using them for illegal activities. That is one headache that you don't want to deal with.

Non-HOAs

When you're looking for a home for yourself to live in, an HOA community can be a great thing. It will give you the peace of mind that comes with living in a community that has set rules and guidelines. It can also be cheaper to find a home in an HOA although you will need to pay the fees that come with it. Homeowners are also responsible for the bills that come with the HOA, and you could end up paying a lot of money in those bills.

If you are only looking for a home to invest in and to flip, an HOA is not going to be your best option. HOAs are notorious for problems that owners end up being responsible for. Since you technically own the home even though you only want to use it as an investment property, you will end up paying the bills in a community that you aren't even a part of. Some HOA's don't even allow flippers to purchase the home unless they are planning to live in the property for a long time.

Investors who want to purchase the home to flip and to then rent out will likely not even be able to do that in an HOA. Most HOAs have rules against this and do not allow rental properties in the community at all because it can bring down the value of other homes.

While properly maintained HOAs and great reputation areas could be a possibility for flippers, it is usually best for investors to just stay away from HOAs. Be sure to look into the property before you buy to make sure that it is not a part of a home owner's association and that you will not be responsible for the costs that come with that.

Chapter 3: Find Deals to Convert Your Investment

The less money that you have to spend on the property and the subsequent flip of the property, the more money you will be able to make. If you are able to get a good deal on the money that you spent, you can increase your profit margin and this will allow you the chance to make even more money from the properties that you have and that you purchase in the future. It is a good idea to always save as much money as you can and to try to get deals on both the actual property and the construction part of the flipping process.

Properties

Every month, there are new property catalogs that are put out in different areas. These are meant for future homeowners to be able to look at to see what they want to purchase and if there is anything that interests them. While you may not be planning on living in the property, you can still get an idea of what is out there and available to you. Even if you don't find a property you like, the catalogs are usually free, and you can at least see what the comparative prices are like.

Property auctions are hotspots for property flippers. Auctions allow you to get a great home for a much lower price than market value most of the time. Check out auction websites or other areas that have the auctions on them to get an idea of what type of properties will be up for sale. One downside to auctions is that you probably will not get a chance to walk through the home before you buy, but it is often worth that for the price that you get. An auction that hasn't been heavily advertised may be your best bet if you don't want to get into a bidding war with your competition.

Speaking of your competition, you should use them to help you find a great deal, too. Your competition may know of homes that they did not want but that are still available. They may also have properties that they just aren't able to flip anymore and may be willing to sell to you for a discount. Even though you are in competition with them, it is a good idea to keep lines of communication open between each other.

You may be surprised but friends and family members might have the information that you need to find your first truly great flip. Check with your friends and family members first. They could be selling their own home or they could know someone who is. Knowing someone may not necessarily help you save any money on the home because they still need to sell it but it may help you to find something that you wouldn't have had the chance to see otherwise. They could be your best resource especially when you are first starting out with your flipping business.

If you are truly serious about getting into property investment, you may be sitting on the best property possible. Homeowners can flip their own home before they begin their business. Doing this will give you the capital that you need to get started and get your property investment business off of the ground. One of the best parts about flipping your own property is that you have likely already put money into it and you may not have to worry about some of the problems that come with purchasing a new property. You will even know ahead of time the problems that the home has.

Materials

The materials that you use for your investment property can begin to take a toll on your budget. Finding a good deal on labor and on materials is almost as important as finding a good deal on a home that you are going to flip. The materials that you use should be high-quality, but they should also not cut very far into your budget. Make sure that you find materials and labor that straddle the fine line between being inexpensive and being a very low quality that could appear cheap to potential buyers.

If you plan on getting into the property investment business, it is a good idea to form a working relationship with a wholesaler. You may need a business license or even a membership fee to be able to get materials at a wholesale price, but the fee will almost always be worth the money that you save especially if you are planning on flipping a lot of properties. Just make sure that you are working with a reputable wholesaler who is not going to sell you items that are damaged, stolen or otherwise compromised. Buying at wholesale can also void the warranty that comes with these items.

It is often worth checking out clearance materials. Make sure that they are on clearance for no reason other than they simply didn't sell. They should not be damaged. While most clearance items do not sell because they are an unpopular color or style, you may get lucky and find a very popular material that was just ordered in excess. If you are considering buying materials on clearance, always find out why, exactly, it is on clearance. It is also a good idea to find out if buying it on clearance could void the warranty on the item.

Another way that you can save money is to buy products at full price. High-quality products that are set at regular price will be able to save you money if you buy the products that are the middle of the line. You don't want to buy the top of the line because they will not pay off in the end and may end up looking ubiquitous in a home that you are trying to sell. You also don't want anything from the bottom of the line because the materials are often cheap and could compromise the quality of the home.

While they are not the most important part of your flip and will certainly not eat up your entire budget, there are things that you must take into consideration when it comes to your materials. Materials will probably not be the most expensive part of your flip and should be treated as just that: materials. Make sure that you purchase ones that your contractor can work with and that you feel comfortable with selling to your potential buyers. Save the majority of your renovation budget to pay the contractor who will be the most expensive part of the flip aside from buying the home.

Labor

It is imperative for your flip that you find someone who will be able to do the labor to make your property beautiful and able to sell. Be sure to find a contractor who is able to provide you with high-quality work that will go along with what you are offering to your potential buyers. A good contractor can be the difference between spending months on a very expensive project and getting it done for a low cost within a few weeks. The labor will eat up a large chunk of your renovation budget so make sure that you are paying for quality.

When it comes to contractors, you need to make sure that the person who is doing your labor is licensed to do so. Someone who is licensed has a good reputation and can provide you with excellent services will be better for you when you are doing your renovation project. A great contractor will also be able to secure the permits and legal paperwork that you need to be able to flip the property in the best way possible so that you can make a profit from the investment.

Unless you are a general contractor by trade, you will probably not be able to do all of the work on your investment property and, even then, you will still need to find specialists who can help you with the property and flipping it the right way. Make sure that you find someone who is reputable and someone who has a lot of experience. This will reduce some of the headache that comes with flipping properties and can make the actual construction process easier for you. Find a great general contractor that you can use on all of your subsequent flips.

Once you have done a few flips and have used the same contractor with great results, you may want to consider starting a partnership with that contractor. This would mean that the contractor works only for you and that they are there for you whenever you need them to start on a home. Partnerships can get messy and can even cause you to lose out on money, though, so make sure that you have established your investment business before you try to start a partnership with a contractor for your properties. Establish yourself before you bring someone else into the mix.

If you are able to get a good deal on the home, on the labor and even on the materials, you will be able to save money when it comes to the property that you are flipping. The more money you are able to save, the better. Make sure that you are getting the highest profit possible by getting great deals on your investment. Always go for quality, though. If you get low quality materials or low quality work, you may end up paying more in the future to fix it before you are able to sell the property.

Chapter 4: Quickly Evaluating Deals

When you are first getting started, it may seem easy to think that you are getting a great deal on a home just because it has a low price, but buyer beware. A low price on a home could signal problems, and you need to make sure that you are truly getting a deal before you make the decision to flip the home. Be sure to take each of these things into account before you purchase the home. The more that you flip homes as investments, the more easily it will be for you to determine whether something is truly a deal or not.

Cost of the Home

The cost of the home is the base price that you are looking at the home for. This is what the home is listed at and what you can expect to pay for the home if you are paying in cash.

There may be other things that are associated with the home, such as closing costs. This will be added to the cost of the home when you are figuring it out for the sake of a budget and for figuring out if you are getting a deal or not.

Make sure that you know the cost of other homes in the area. If the home is comparable to those, this may be a great buy for you. If it is far below the value of other homes in the area, retreat! It may be so low because there are problems with it. By looking at other comparative homes in the area, you will have a good idea of what you should be paying. As long as the home does not have many more bedrooms or is a completely different design as the other homes, you should only pay around the same amount as what other homes are.

When you are looking at the cost of the home, only consider the actual cost of the home. It may be handy for you to make a spreadsheet or a chart that you can fill in when you are looking at homes that could, potentially, become your next flip. Fill in the cost of the home in the area that you have set aside for that. You can create another line for the mortgage and the subsequent interest payments so do not include that in the cost of the home line.
There may be other costs that are associated with the home. Consider using a document research company to help you find out if there are any liens on the home or any back taxes. These could be hefty and could add a lot

of money to the cost of the home. If you know whether or not these are going to be on the home upfront, you will not have to worry about losing any money from them out of your contingency budget.

Mortgage

Unless you have the cash to pay for your investment properties upfront, you are going to need a mortgage for the home. If you plan on paying cash, feel free to jump to the next section but stay in this chapter.

The mortgage is going to cost you a lot of money when you are renovating the home. You will need a down payment for the mortgage. Understand how much that is. You can choose to include that either in your home cost or in the mortgage cost. Either one will work but beware this is the only thing that can cross boundaries between the two lines of your budget.

Find out what you will be paying in an interest rate. The interest rate should be calculated based on the home price and anything else that you include in the mortgage. If you have gotten a 15-year mortgage, divide the total interest cost (can be found by multiplying the total interest amount by the interest rate and subtracting the down payment) by 15. Divide it again by 12. That will tell you what the exact interest will be costing you each month. Add that to the line.

If you would rather see it all together, find out what your mortgage payment will be each month. It may save you some time and some math to just figure this out. Give it its own line on your budget. Do not put a mortgage payment and an interest payment in a budget together. Choose one or the other. When you are first getting started with your flipping business, it will be

much easier for you to just see what the mortgage is when you look at your budget.
Use the contractor that you are using for the next step. Find out how long he or she thinks the project is going to take. Ask them the worst case scenario and be generous when you are figuring it out. For example, you can add a month or two onto the total time so that you are completely sure that you will not end up over budget.

Renovation Costs

Your renovation is going to cost a lot of money. Be prepared to pay more than what you initially thought for the renovation and make sure that you know what you are getting yourself into. Ask your contractor to give you the price that he or she is going to expect the project to cost before you even begin the work on the house. Ideally, you should ask them before you even buy the house.

Somethings that you should take into consideration when you are looking at the renovation are any structural changes, permit costs, and cosmetic updates to the property. Remember that there is an inside and an outside to every property. You don't want to neglect one or the other because that can have a damaging effect on the resale of the home.

Your contractor will tell you what he or she expects you to pay for the project. Set aside a little more than that in your budget so that you are able to handle any surprises that may come up while you are working on the project. This should be different than the contingency that the contractor has set.

Consider having an inspector look at the home before you purchase or require the seller to give you an inspection report. This will allow you to be more secure in the fact that there are no structural damages. You should expect to have some minor issues with the structure of the home especially if it is a really old home. If the home requires a brand new electrical and plumbing system and it has rotting boards holding it up, you probably don't want to buy that home.

A great contractor will always have a contingency in their renovation budget. This is an amount of money that they will include the cost of your project that will be set aside for the unknown. This money can usually be used for things that crop up during the renovation. Most often, it is enough to cover one big project that comes up or several small ones. If there are many problems with the home, you may go through your contingency quickly which can become a big problem for your budget.

Keep in mind that your renovation budget should be worst case scenario. Create a line for the renovation on the budget that you have created for yourself. Make sure that only renovation costs go onto this line and that you are able to look at it clearly to see what you can expect to pay for the renovation. This may seem like a relatively small step, but it may end up being the most amount of money that you pay throughout the entire project. If you budget correctly, you will be able to more clearly see if you are getting a deal on the property.

Sale Costs

Unless you have ever sold a home before, you may be surprised to learn that it isn't exactly free to sell your home. There are a lot of costs that can come with the sale of the home.
If you are not a realtor or do not have one that is specifically employed by your investment property company, you should consider getting a real estate license. This can save you a huge amount of money when you are selling the home and can be worth it in the end. Only consider this if you are truly serious about the investment property business.

Commission is one thing that most people do not consider when they are selling their flipped home. If you use a realtor to sell your home, you will be required to pay them a commission on the home that you have sold. Commission is a portion of the sale of the home, usually 10% or less, and is how realtors get paid. They have likely done a lot of work to help you sell your home, and you need to consider what the commission will be when you are looking at the budget and whether or not the home is a deal.

If you have done any type of renovation work on the home, you will need to have it inspected before you try to sell it. Not only is it the law in most states, but having an inspection report readily available for your potential buyers will help you sell the home more quickly. If you have used a reputable contractor to do the renovations, you will have nothing to worry about when it comes to your inspection. You will even be able to save some money if everything was done the right way.

The last thing that you need to think about are the other closing costs of the home that are unrelated to realtor comission. Most of the time, the seller is required to pay them. Since it is not often that you can get a buyer who is willing to pay them or even negotiate it in a part of a deal on the home, you need to consider these costs when you are looking at the total price of the home. While closing costs may seem like a small inconvenience, they can actually be quite expensive. Make sure that you are aware of what the average closing costs would be. Consult your realtor to find out what they will be based on what you are going to sell the home for.

While it may seem complicated with all of the steps, it is actually quite easy. Find out how much the house will cost you for the entire project, how much you will be paying for the renovation, and any sale costs that you are likely to incur. Subtract all of that by a reasonable comparative price for renovated homes in the area, and you will have the number that tells you whether or not you are getting a deal.

Chapter 5: Making a Competitive Offer

Now that you have found the home that you want to invest in, you have figured out that it is a great deal and you have secured the financing that you need to be able to purchase it, you may be eager to jump onto it as quickly as possible. That type of gusto will help you, but you also need some help to beat out the other competition on the home. Chances are, you won't have much time to make an offer to the seller.

Get Friendly

One of the easiest things that you can do in business to get people to like you is to simply be likable. What does that mean, though? It means that you need to be as friendly as possible. Get out there and be friendly with the sellers of the home. Be kind, be respectful and let them know that you love the home. While you may be eager to mention it, don't let them know that you are planning on flipping their beloved home.

Believe it or not, sellers can actually refuse your offer with no reason. As long as they are discriminating against you in the form of one of the protected categories, they can choose any reason that they would like not to sell the home to you. Even if you have the highest offer, the only place that will guarantee you a home is an auction. Be as likeable as possible so that the sellers will want to sell to you.

A word of caution: don't be fake. Most people can see right through you. You genuinely want to buy the home so try to be as genuine as possible in the way that you talk to the sellers and the different things that you have to say to them. It may be hard, at first, but you will eventually learn how to be kind and friendly without overdoing it or feeling like you are piling up the sweet words. One thing that could help you is remembering that you getting the home is based on how much they like you. It may make it easier to be nice to them.

If you are finding it very difficult to be friendly to the sellers of the home, consider sending your real estate agent in to look at the home for you. He or she has been professionally trained to be a charmer, and that will likely help you get the home.

Remember, being friendly is only the first step toward making the seller choose you and getting the home that you want to be able to renovate. There are much more things that are involved but setting up the framework with a positive attitude, and a friendly demeanor will only help you.

Stand Out

Don't show up at the open house with your favorite Cyndi Lauper workout gear and a very loud mouth, but make an effort to stand out to the seller. While we have been taught our entire lives to try to conform, it may be a good thing to stand out to the seller. He or she will remember you more when they are considering the offer.

A great business tactic that you can use when you are trying to seal the deal and make a competitive offer is to make an emotional connection with the buyer. Appeal to them. If you see a photo of their pets or kids, inquire about them. Mention that you have nieces or nephews that you just adore, too. Don't lie to try to make the connection but do try to find something that you feel you will truly be able to connect with them on. If you just take a look around the house, it will be easy for you to find something that you can connect with them about and do it. Making an emotional connection may be the thing that stands out in their memory when they are considering your offer.

To help you stand out to the seller, ask them what their favorite part of the home is. Most people have a favorite part of their own home, and you can appeal to them by taking their feelings into account. If you have not seen that part of the home yet, ask them to show it to you so that you will be able to see their reaction to the favorite part. Try your best to see what they love so much about it and let them know that you understand why they like that area.

It may be tempting to bring along a fruit basket or cookies because who doesn't love food? Don't do it, though. Not only will sellers see this as somewhat of a plea for them to choose you and think that you are desperate, but it may actually be illegal in some areas. No matter how small the gift is, it may be considered a bribe. The only thing that you should feel compelled to bring is your game face to beat out the competition and your friendliness to appeal to the seller of the house so that you can score that deal.

Don't Take too Long

Once you have made an offer on a home, you have 15 days to get someone to inspect the home before you make the decision on whether you truly want to buy it. This gives you the assurance that you need to make the right choice for your home. People who are buying homes to live in are able to use this time to get things in order and to make sure that they are getting the best home possible and that there are no problems with it. This is not a good idea if you are buying the home to flip.

Try to bring your contractor or someone else who can inspect the property along with you to the showing of the home. He or she will be able to tell you what they think will need to be done and what you can expect after you have actually purchased the property. While this will not be as thorough as an official inspection of the home, it will be able to save you some time when it comes to the way that you can purchase the home. This time could be spent with you getting the house instead of letting it go to someone else who is not going to take as long.

Just because you have the full 15 days does not mean that you need to use it. Consider only using around 5 days at the most so that you will be able to get your offer in first and that you will be able to actually secure the house with what you are going to pay for it with. This is much easier if you are paying with cash or you do not need to go through a lender to get the deal on the house. You need to make sure that you have your finances in order before you even make an offer on the house. Know what you are going to pay for the house and make sure that you stick with it when you go to the open house. Know how much money you have to spend and what your cutoff will be. By doing this, you will buy yourself some time. While other potential buyers are still trying to figure out how they are going to pay for the house, you may be drawing on the mortgage and getting the house of your dreams.

Shoot High

The seller has set the price of the house for a reason. Either he or she has an emotional attachment to it or they think that it is truly worth the amount that they are asking. Likely, their realtor advised them on what they should sell the house for and this is what they have listed it at. This is often in comparison to other houses in the area and is something that will be right in line with the median price for that type of home in the state as well as the specific region that the home is in.

Don't offend the seller with a lowball offer. If you think that the home needs a lot of extra work, consider bringing that point up at the open house. The seller may be ignorant to that fact and may consider lowering the price. If you do not get anywhere by doing this, you need to just move on. Finding a different house will be a better option than trying to get the house for a very low price, offending the seller and making a bad name for yourself in the real estate community. You are trying to build up your home investment business, not tear it down when you are looking at your very first property.

It is a good idea to offer the seller exactly what he or she is asking for the house. You should make your offer based on the list price, and it really shouldn't be any lower than the list price. This is the price that you figured your budget up with, anyway, so it should not make a difference if you have to pay the full price for your house. Most of the time, if a seller gets a full price offer on the home that they are trying to sell, they will take it right away. Try to get your offer in before any of the other buyers who are trying to get the home, too. Your offer being the first could secure the home for you.

If you absolutely must, go slightly above the list price. A good idea to figure out whether or not you should do this is to see how many people are interested in the house. Go to the open house at a prime time and see how many other people are there. If there are many people there, try to judge their reactions. You should offer just above list price if it seems like a lot of people are interested in the home. The other time that this is acceptable is when the home is for sale in a seller's market.

Unless you must have the home right then or there is no another option for you, you should not go very far above list price. If you are having a hard time finding a house to flip that you don't have to offer an outrageous amount of money on top of the list price, you may want to consider branching out to a different area to flip houses and invest in houses in.

Chapter 6: Use Time Management for Your Benefit

When you are doing any type of project, it is always a good idea to do your best to manage your time so that you will be able to get the most out of the time that you spend on a project. You should make sure that when you are flipping houses or working on investment properties, that you manage your time as wisely as you possibly can. This will help you to be more successful with your time and can even allow you to increase your profit margin on the homes that you are flipping.

Work on Big Projects First

One of the first rules of time management is to tackle the daunting tasks first so that the smaller tasks will feel minor in comparison. If you make sure that you work on the big house projects first, you will be able to be more prepared for the smaller things. Bonus: some of the smaller things may actually get done while you are working on bigger projects out of necessity.

If you have something like plumbing or electrical that needs to be replaced, have, your contractors do that work first. This will be one of the biggest parts of the project and will likely require you to tear down portions of the inside of the house. If you start with these, you can avoid having to tear down walls that you just pained or installed new cabinetry in. By doing these big things first, you will make sure that you don't have to backtrack on the work that you did or have to completely redo it since you had to tear walls down.

While it may be tempting because it can make a huge difference in a home, don't ever start with the painting. The paint on your home should be the very last thing that is done and should be done by contracted painters. Even when you are at the very end of your project, you do not know if you will have to pull an outlet out of a wall or make adjustments on a wall that was just painted. By making paint the last thing that you do, you will save yourself some grief at the very end of the project.

Set a Time Limit

Each section of the home should have a time limit on it. Your contractor will probably set a time limit for his people to be done in each area of the home but keep in mind that they will probably go over that time limit.

By setting your own time limit, you will be able to be prepared when they go on their own. Consider adding around 10% of the time that they have said that they were going to be done with a project. For example, if your contractor says that a project will be done in 10 days, add an extra day on so that you won't be sorely disappointed when they go over.

The more homes you invest in, the more likely you will be able to know whether a time limit is going to be realistic. Talk with your contractor before they start on the home and get their idea of what the length of time the work will take is. They will have the best idea because they are accustomed to doing work like that and they know how long it takes each of their subcontractors to be able to do the work for them.

If things do not get done in a certain amount of time, push your contractor to get his crews to work more efficiently. There is always work that can be done. Your general contractor should be working as hard as possible to get this done as quickly as possible. As long as you have let him or her know that you are trying to flip the property, they should know that your profit (and their payment) depends on how quickly they can get things done. A time limit will help them to know that they are under pressure to get things done as quickly as possible.

Create a Contingency Time Budget

You have a contingency budget for your finances so why not have one for the time that is going to be spent on the project? Adding expected time to the project will make an overdue project less of a blow on the stress that you will already have surrounding the home and the flipping process. If you have a contingency in place for a time, you will be able to use that up when your contractors let you know that they are not going to get things done as quickly as what you thought they were originally going to get it done.

The contingency time budget is something that will work wonders for the stress that you feel when you are flipping homes. Your contractors may not know that you have built a few extra days in, but you will know that. They will continue to work hard, but you will have the satisfaction of knowing that you will have extra time if something goes wrong.

One of the easiest ways that you can do this is to schedule your open house around two weeks after your contractor's expected end date. If the project is done before, simply move your open house up which is much easier than trying to push it back.

Work With Contractors

You don't necessarily need to get down and dirty with the contractors who are working on your home but do everything that you can to be able to help them out with the project. If they need permits, give them the information that they need to be able to take to the city. If they need paperwork from you, make it a priority. Your contractor is trying to work as quickly as possible so that your project will get done as quickly as possible. Don't make their job harder.

If there are small things that you can do to help the contractor, like carrying in supplies for painters or helping to screw on electrical outlet plates, do it. You may be paying for them to do everything when it comes to the renovation, but there is nothing saying that you can't help. Remember, the more bodies the contractors have done work, the faster the project will be able to get done. If your project gets done before you were planning, you will be able to make more profits on it and much more quickly than what you have set out to do.

Even though your contractor is technically hired help, you should not treat them as such. You should be a team player and work with them to make sure that things are getting done the right way. There are many things that you will be able to do to help out your contractor. Simply ask them if there is anything that you can do to help get the project done quickly.

Consider a Project Manager

One of the easiest things that you can do to manage your time is to get someone else who is able to do it for you. A project manager is that person, and they will be able to provide you with the help that you need when it comes to handling your contractor and everything else throughout the renovation.

A professional project manager will be able to assess the situation that your renovation is in and take things over for you. The only thing that you will need to do is sign off on major changes and, initially, let the project manager know what you want to be done to the house while people are working on it.

Make sure that you only hire a project manager when you are ready. A manager can be expensive and can eat into the budget that you have set for your flip. If you are just getting started with flipping houses and investment properties, you probably don't need a project manager. Try your hardest to manage your time on your own and make sure that you are doing things the right way. Once you have flipped a lot of houses, have made a lot of money and have more than one property that you are working on at a time, you may want to consider hiring a project manager for each of your investment properties.

Chapter 7: Hiring the Right Team for the Project

The right team can be the difference between having a flip that makes you a lot of money and a flip that makes you lose a lot of money. While you don't necessarily have to hire a huge crew of people who can help you out with your project, you will want to hire the right people who can make things right for your investment property. The right team can truly help you make more money and increase your profit margin on the home.

Realtor

Your realtor should be able to get the house that you want for the price you want but also sell the house that you have created for the price that you want to sell it for.

This is something that they need to be able to do and finding the right one can make a huge difference in your investment property.

It is always a good idea to find a realtor who has a great reputation and one who has worked with investors in the past because they will know how to handle your situation in the best way possible.

Make sure that when you hire your real estate agent, you let them know that you are planning to flip houses for a profit. Your intentions as an investor should always be clear to your real estate agent. This will give him or her a better chance at looking at houses for you. Finding houses for an investor is much different than finding ones for someone who wants to actually live in the home.

To find a great realtor, consider simply calling around to find out which ones are the best ones for investors. If a Realtor does not have any experience working with an investor, step away. You may be able to save a lot of money by using someone who has not worked with investors before, but it will not be worth it.

A good investment real estate agent will be able to help you find homes that are inexpensive, can be easily flipped and are in areas that have a high cash flow. The right one will know how to do each of these things to ensure that you are getting the best house to be able to invest in. The right realtor will also give you plenty of options to choose from.

Contractor

With the right contractor, your home will get done more quickly than if you used someone who had no experience with investment properties. A good contractor will have worked on investment properties before and will have the right crew to be able to do the job. Most contractors also come with their own pick of subcontractors that they have used before and have had good results with in the past.

When a contractor is working on a home that someone is going to live in, he or she is still on a time limit. If the project is not finished in time, it is an inconvenience to the homeowner. When a contractor is working on a home that someone is trying to flip for a profit, it is imperative that they meet the time requirements. If the project is not finished in time, it will cost the investor possibly thousands of dollars in profit since they will have to continue paying a mortgage on the home while the project is being finished. Contractors who have worked with investors before will know this. Contractors who have only worked with homeowners before may have trouble grasping this idea.
All contractors believe that the people they use to do different jobs are the best in the business, but an established contractor will have a crew of people that he or she works with on a regular basis and are truly good. They will have quality work and will be able to provide your investment property with the work that it deserves. This is something that is very important because these are the people who are going to be taking care of all of the changes that are happening to your home.

Subcontractors
Even though your general contractor trusts the chosen subcontractors, that does not mean that you have to trust them, too. It is a good idea to get to know your

subcontractors before they begin working on your home. Ask for samples of their work and find out from your contractor why he or she likes them so much. If there is something that you do not like, consider trying to find other ones. Your general contractor will likely have contacts with other people who will be able to help you find subcontractors who are just perfect for your investment property.

All subcontractors should have samples of the work that they have done. They should be willing to show them to you. It is a good idea to do a quick check of their credentials before you make the decision to allow your general contractor to hire them to work on your project. You never know what may be lurking under the surface of what seems like a great business. Make sure that they are efficient at what they do, too. You don't want your entire project to be held up because your plumber doesn't even know how to install a new commode.

Something that you may not know is that you can hire your general contractor without accepting the work of his or her chosen subcontractors. You need to be happy with all of the work that is being done on your home and if the subcontractors are not providing that to you, feel free to fire them and replace them with a company that you like better. Just because the general contractor that you have hired likes a certain company does not mean that you will need to use that company for your project. Your general contractor should understand that you would prefer to use someone that you like better.

Inspectors

In some locations, you may not be able to choose the inspector that you get to check out your home, but you should still hire your own private inspector to look at the home and make sure that everything is done the way that it is supposed to be. It is important that you do this so that you will know what is going to happen before the state or city inspects the property.

Your contractor should know the names of inspectors who can look at your property. They can refer you to them so that you will be able to get the most out of the situation.

It is a good idea to have the inspection done well in advance of the open house in case anything comes up with the property or you need to change something that is not up to code. Your inspector will be able to tell you what needs to be changed, if anything, long before you are set to show the home to potential buyers. The inspector should also be there before your final inspection with the city.

While most private inspectors do not work for the city, they are familiar with all of the codes and everything that you must have in place to be able to pass the municipal inspection. Make sure that you listen to the inspector and make the changes that you need to make before you have the home available as an open house to potential buyers. A home that needs major changes done to it before people can buy it after they have already seen the home will not be a hot seller.

Stagers

One thing that many property investors forget about on their first flip is the way that the inside of the home looks. When you are selling the home that you have lived in, your furniture and belongings work well for the open houses. They make the home appear to be lived in, and that is what people want to see. When you have flipped a home, unless you have flipped your own home, you are not going to have any of those belongings there in the home with you. That is where the stagers come in to help you out.

Stagers are people that will come into your home and will set up furniture, tchotchkes, and other décor that will make the newly renovated home look like it is lived in. They are experts in design, and many of them were interior designers before they began staging homes. They have many pieces that they can put into your home and the right stager will know just what to do for your home. From using neutral tones to baking cookies before the open houses, the stagers can set the mood for selling the home.

Some stagers do such a good job that people may ask if there is an option to purchase the furniture with the house. This is something that you will need to discuss with your stager before the open house and before anyone has a chance to see it. Most of the furniture that stagers use is only on loan to you – that is what you pay them for in addition to their style expertise. Some stagers may have the option for buyers to purchase the furniture when they buy the home. This would be a separate transaction from what you would sell the home for so get this information from your stager. Always have their business card ready to hand out to your potential clients who love the setup of the home.

Help your stager out, and he or she will help you. Remember, staging is sometimes the single thing that sells your home's

Chapter 8: Speeding Up Your Flip

The faster you get your flip done, the more money you stand to make. You will have to pay much less in mortgage payments, and you may even be able to avoid some of them altogether when you are able to finish your flip ahead of schedule. Now, how can you do this without sacrificing the quality of work that comes with taking your time? You don't have to sacrifice anything.

Offer Incentives
Your general contractor and the crews that they have will work faster if there is something that they are looking forward to at the end of the project. Anyone can work for a paycheck, only the truly motivated will work for a pizza party or some extra cash thrown their way. This should not cost you too much, but an extra hundred dollars can mean a lot to the people who are doing the work on your home. Well-fed manual laborers always seem to work more efficiently, too.

Make sure that the incentives that you offer are not going to cut too much into your budget. If you offer too high of an incentive that costs you too much money, the money that you save on fewer mortgage payments will not be worth it in the end and may end up being much more expensive than if you would have just let the crews finish on time.

It is important to note that the quicker they work, the more likely they will be to make mistakes. For this reason, you don't want the project to be finished too quickly. The project getting finished ahead of schedule will not be worth it if the crews have to take extra time to go back and fix all of the mistakes that they made while they were hastily working away to be able to earn that pizza you brought in for them. Fast is good, but speeding up too much can cause major problems with your flip.

Get Your Hands Dirty

It was your idea to flip the home. You likely have, at least, a small amount of experience working in homes or doing some type of renovation or this is not something that you would have chosen. Even if you don't have any experience, anyone is able to tear down old wallpaper, clean up debris or change out light bulbs in all of the rooms throughout the house. Consider getting your own hands dirty to help finish the project more quickly. Some of the things that you can do:

Small demolition projects
Wallpaper removal
Trimming the paint in a room
Pulling weeds for curb appeal
Putting the finishing touches on a staging job
Helping your contractors with small jobs
Going around and cleaning everything as projects are completed

All of these things are very easy and do not require you to have a lot of skills to be able to do. Feel free to start these on your own. It is your house after all. If you find something that needs to be done and it looks like you can do it, go ahead and do it. This is something that will be helpful to the contractors and will help speed up the process of renovating the home. Only do projects that you know will not affect the outcome negatively. Foolproof things like putting in light bulbs and sweeping the kitchen will not mess the project up.

Before you try to do anything, talk with your contractor. He or she may be keeping the light switch plates off for a reason. Get their advice and know what they are doing with the project. You may even consider asking them what you can help with. They likely have very many small jobs that need to be done to help finish your property. Doing these are easy for you but can greatly speed up the process of renovating the home and push your home much closer to completion and the subsequent open house of the property.

By doing all of these things, you will not only be able to speed up the process of getting your home done, but you will also be able to learn more about what it is like to be on the other side of completing a home. Make sure that you do everything that you can while you are doing this so that you will be able to get things done more quickly.

Don't Cut Corners

Saving time by skipping a few steps may seem like a good idea, but it will end up costing you much more time in the long run.

When you cut corners on your renovation project, you are risking ruining the entire thing because you were too impatient to wait until it was truly time to unveil the newly renovated house. Cutting corners may seem like a good idea for a DIY project on your own home, but you are now a professional who is trying to make the properties an investment for yourself. Don't cut corners to save money, time or for any reason at all. You will end up paying for it at some point during your project.

Combine Steps

While you should not cut corners in your investment renovation, there are some things that you can do to combine steps and save on the time that it takes you to complete the project.

One of the most common things that people do when they are preparing their home for an open house is doing the touchups in the home during the time that the stagers are setting things up. As long as you stay out of the way of where they are doing their job, you can do things like add switch plates and touch up the paint around the trim.

There are other steps to your renovation that can be combined, too. If you have the budget to pay for it and really want to speed things up, consider talking to your general contractor about hiring more people on the crew. This will allow them to work in one area of the home while there is another project going on in a different area of the home. By doing this, you will be able to speed the project up, and you can take up to half the time that it would have taken to finish the project.

You can do a lot of these things on your own, but it is important to check with your contractor. He or she may have better ideas on how to speed things up and what can be done. When you are first securing the general contractor to use on the project, let them know that you want to move as fast as possible to get the house done. This will let them know ahead of time what you are looking for and they may be able to work faster or implement other options that will allow the project to go more quickly.

If you let your general contractor know after they have already been working on the house, there are still some things that they will be able to do. They want to be done with the project quickly, too so that they can make more money on the next project. You may be surprised to find that they did not even know that you wanted them to work very fast on the project. If you let them know what you want from them, they can make the project faster and can do a better job than if you had just assumed that they would be moving fast to get it done.

Speeding up the process always seems like a good idea because it will allow you to reach the completion of your project more quickly, but you must consider the different aspects that go into working faster. If you do not have contractors who are comfortable with working fast, do not push them to work faster. This will result in work that is sloppy, not finished or not done the right way. Make sure that your contractors are comfortable with working fast and that they can do it the right way.

There is no point in speeding up the process of flipping a home unless it is done the right way the first time to actually save you time on the project.

Chapter 9: Flipping Quickly

At the beginning of your flipping career, you should not aim to do things quickly. You should focus more on getting it done and getting it done the right way so that you will be able to have high-quality homes that people will want to move into once you have finished the project. Once you get comfortable with your skills on investment properties, you can then start trying to move faster to get things done.

The Benefits

There are many benefits that come with flipping a home quickly but one of the biggest things that will result is that you will be done with it sooner and you will be able to start trying to make a profit on it while you are working in the different areas. The quicker that you get it done, the more likely you will be to walk away from home in the black instead of in the red.

Until you actually sell the home, you are not making any profit. You are only driving yourself further into a loss on the home. This is a problem for many flippers and something that you will likely encounter, at least, once in your flipping career. You will probably even have a home or two that you do not profit from at all. It is not uncommon for investment properties to end up being a loss and this can be something that is difficult to deal with. Don't let it get you down and try to move onto the next project and do things differently so that you can make a profit on those.

Another major benefit that comes with flipping projects quickly is that you will be able to save more money on the mortgage. Unless you paid for the home in cash, every day that you are working on the house, it costs you money. This can be a huge hit to your budget and can cause you to suffer a lot of loss of money. By finishing the projects as quickly as possible, you have a shorter time that you are paying the mortgage, or paying to hold onto the home while it is being completed.

The Results

The result of a quicker flipped home will be noticeable and will draw more people in. People who saw the home in its former condition will be interested in what you did and how you did it so quickly.

A home that is flipped more quickly will be able to sell faster, too. This is because it will be completed and will be ready to go back on the market in a shorter period of time than if it was still being renovated and still taking a long time to complete. Make sure that you know what you are doing when you are speeding things up so that the home will be in the best shape possible. The results will show both your commitment to completing the home quickly and doing it the right way for your potential buyers.

The home that you flip should have a lot of appeal to it, both from the curb and inside. If you work hard and fast on the home, you will be able to have both of these things so that you are able to do more with it and so that more people will be interested in seeing the home. It will be better for your investment business.

One thing that is a good idea is to take before pictures of the home. You may not want to show these when you are doing your open house because it can actually be a deterrent to buyers, but some people may be interested in what the home looked like in the past. By taking before pictures, you will also have something that you can add to your portfolio. This will help you later on down the road if you decide that you want to flip homes for other people or do it for someone other than yourself.

How To

The most important part of flipping houses in a short period of time so that you can make more profit is learning how to actually do it.

By combining your own best efforts, the effort of your team and excellent business practices, you will be able to make your flips go quicker and smoother. The number one thing that you can do to do this is practice. The more flips that you do, the better you and your team will get at flipping and the faster you will all be able to work on the projects that you have set out to complete.

Be organized. You will not be able to get anywhere with your renovation projects if you are not organized and prepared to make the most out of the project. It is a good idea to have a checklist of everything that you must do when you are looking for the property, renovating the property and selling the property. Being organized will help reduce the amount of time that you would spend preparing to do the project and will help you to do your flips much faster.

As you become more comfortable with your general contractor and the people who are working on the home, you will learn the way that they work and what they are able to do in different amounts of time. Learn how they work and what their strengths are. Encourage them to do the same thing as you and get organized. If you have been working with your contractor for a while, check in to make sure that he or she has a checklist or an order that everything is done in. Contractors should be just as organized as you so that they don't have to waste time planning out what order they are going to do the project in.

The business aspect of investing in homes can take up a lot of your time, but if you do it the right way, you will be able to get the project done much faster. Always follow the best business practices when you are securing financing, going through the purchase process and even paying your contractors. If you pay promptly, you will be able to save yourself some time. As you get deeper into the business of flipping houses, you will find that you will have more funds to be able to pay people sooner to do the work.

Selling It

When you take a long time to sell the home, you will lose more money on it. It is a good idea to sell to the person who is offering the highest amount as quickly as possible.

The first highest offer may come the day of your open house or even weeks after. If people are offering far below the list price of the home, you may have it set too high. Make a quick adjustment on the price of the home and see more offers come floating in. If someone offers you list price on the home, you should absolutely take it. Don't wait for someone to offer above list price because that day may never come and you may end up losing the full list price offer that you just received.

Cash offers are always king when it comes to selling the home. If someone is offering you cash for the home, but they want to pay slightly below the list price, take that offer. Cash deals can be handled faster than their mortgage counterparts, and you will be able to close on the house in a shorter period of time. You may be surprised to find just how many people are willing to offer you cash for the home that you have just flipped.

Some home sellers like to take their emotions into account when they are selling. You don't have the luxury to do this because you need to sell the home for a profit. You shouldn't have any emotional attachments to the home, and you should be able to unload it off of yourself as quickly as possible so that you can begin reaping the benefits of all of the hard work that you put in.

Reputation

Your reputation as a business person is so important in the world of investment properties. You need to make sure that people see you as a good flipper and not as someone who rips people off with the houses that you have completed. You could be surprised to find that you will have an easier time selling houses if you have a good reputation than you would if you have continuously ripped people off in the time that you have been in business. Make sure that you know what you are doing when you are renovating the home to help you save time.

If you have a poor reputation in the investment community, you will not be able to sell your houses as quick. People who know you and have seen shoddy work in the past will spread the word around that your flips are terrible and that you do not do a good job. This will cause people to shy away from your open houses and not want to purchase from you. It can be hard to build a good reputation but just make sure that you are not creating a bad reputation for yourself in the process.

Flippers who have an amazing reputation in the investment property sector will be able to sell the properties based just off of their name. If everyone knows your name and knows the work that you do, they will be fighting to buy a home from you. You'll find that people are very interested in the properties that you put up especially if you make sure that you let everyone know that it was you who did the project. A good name in the home renovation industry can make a difference and may be the key to your success.

The most important thing to remember when you are flipping houses is that you *will* get better at it. You will get more comfortable with the process, your crew and even selling the home. You may even find that you enjoy taking on many projects at once to help yourself make more money.

The more homes you do, the easier it will become. You will someday look back at your first home and wonder how you got to where you are. As a successful investor, you will be able to reap the benefits that come from flipping many homes quickly and efficiently.

Part 3 - Real Estate Agent

How to become a successful Real Estate Agent

By Sabi Shepherd

Additionally, the information in the following pages is intended only for informational purposes and should thus be thought of as universal. As befitting its nature, it is presented without assurance regarding its prolonged validity or interim quality. Trademarks that are mentioned are done without written consent and can in no way be considered an endorsement from the trademark holder.

Introduction: The Attitude of a Real Estate Agent

Congratulations on purchasing *Real Estate Agent: How to Become a Successful Real Estate Agent (Volume 3),* and thank you for doing so.

The following chapters will discuss, step-by-step, how to get licensed, promote yourself and your properties, useful tools and tips for real estate agents, and how to adopt the attitude of a successful real estate agent.

There are plenty of books on this subject on the market; thanks again for choosing this one! Every effort was made to ensure it is full of as much useful information as possible. Please enjoy!

Many people enter into their new real estate profession with a mistaken idea of what it will take to become a successful agent. They have seen some of the famous television programs that feature a couple making their buying decision on a million-dollar home purchase after having walked through three homes with the agent. The agent is nowhere to be seen as the couple sits in a neighborhood restaurant over a mimosa and amiably decides on house #2. The next thing you see is the agent meeting with the couple to tell them the good news–they got the house, and everybody lives happily ever after.

If this sounds like the fairytale you've imagined, then your new career in real estate may be doomed before it's had a chance to develop. Not that becoming a real estate agent can't offer incredible opportunities, but the television version of home selling and buying hasn't given you the full picture. Hence, the decision to write this book was made so that you will have a satisfying and fruitful start to your new career as a real estate agent.

Before beginning your step-by-step process of becoming an accomplished real estate agent in today's market, you'll need to adopt an active and productive selling attitude. This attitude of selling is not what many of you might think. It does not depend on your persuasive skills or some slick sales talk. No! The selling attitude is one of unselfishly helping your prospects come to a decision that is right for them and their families. If your eyes are focused on what is best for your clients instead of what is best for your pocketbook, then your business will grow by the word-of-mouth of happy home buyers and sellers.

This book will show you many strategies and techniques to help you help your clients in the process of buying and selling real estate, but if you have a "help yourself" attitude, your sales will suffer, and your job satisfaction will be minimal. Nothing makes one feel better than genuinely helping others find their dream homes. The attitude of an excellent real estate agent is one of customer service, shared knowledge, selling skills, and effective teamwork that results in a positive experience for all parties.

I am a REAL ESTATE AGENT!

You may have heard others say about a person “He was just born to be a salesperson;” however, can you remember seeing a newborn and saying to yourself “Now that one’s going to be a salesperson?” Becoming a real estate professional is a learned skill and one that offers incredible rewards to agents with the right motives and a heart for helping. It requires negotiating skill where everybody is asked to compromise, and yet all parties are happy with the outcome. Those whose negotiations leave some so disgruntled that they leave the table feeling like it was an unfair give and take exchange, often regret the entire experience. Whereas, if your negotiations make everybody feel as though they won, then you’ll not only be more satisfied, but you’ll gain new prospects as well.

Helping your prospects buy or sell real estate requires skills that many agents rarely use—ones like active listening, extensive market knowledge, accurately presenting all the possibilities, and then encouraging clients to come to an agreement. The illustration of what makes a successful salesperson can be seen by the triangle of sales below.

Being a dynamic salesperson requires all three of these elements, but the foundation of your sales will be dependent upon your attitude. It's a known fact that people like doing business with people they like—so, be likable. With some prospects, this can be your greatest challenge. What you'll learn throughout your real estate career is that those clients who are tough, particularly disagreeable, and difficult to win over, will become your most loyal customers who repeatedly provide you with other referrals and ongoing business.

Doing business with Mr. Disagreeable offers exclusive perks you won't experience with other prospects.

- You won't have much competition because no other agents even want to do business with him.
- All his neighbors know how difficult he is to work with, and they consider you quite the salesperson to have successful won him over.
- You have nothing to lose for trying. The worse that can happen is that he bruises your ego a bit and it causes you to grow a tougher exterior, which you'll need throughout your career as a real estate agent.
- You'll learn how to handle the difficult prospects, and you'll get a chance to be the hero.

- You’ll learn how to maintain an attitude of selling through the most difficult of circumstances, and that is a lesson well learned.
- When you have indeed won Mr. Disagreeable over, you'll have a customer for life. As loud and obnoxious as Mr. Disagreeable can be during your early encounters, he'll be just as zealous in sharing all the wonderful things you did for him and become one of your most powerful sources of referrals.
- Having a positive selling attitude can be taught, but maintaining that position with challenging prospects takes practice and the only way to get that practice is to deal with many Mr. Disagreeables.

An imbalance of these skills will give your career as a real estate agent inconsistent results. If your knowledge is excellent, but you lack in skills and your attitude is poor, your sales will be just as one-sided. You will mostly appeal to the analytical types whose primary concern is your market knowledge. A professional agent will be well-rounded, possessing an equal amount of knowledge, skills, and a positive attitude.

If you are still eager to begin your journey to becoming a real estate agent, let's jump right in a get you started on your new career in real estate. From learning the quickest and most efficient way to get licensed, to winning that first listing and showing your first buyers a home, you'll learn the strategies and methods that have created success in today's peak performers.

Chapter 1: Step-by-Step Guide to Getting Licensed

The steps we are going to show you will not only save you time, but it could also make your licensing experience a much more affordable and satisfying process. Be sure to review each step, even if you have already done some preliminary research on the topic, you'll learn some valuable tips on licensing in this chapter.

How Much Will My Real Estate License Cost?

Getting your real estate license could cost you absolutely nothing. With a bit of legwork, some research into the companies you're considering, and some smart negotiations with local designated brokers, and you could be looking at no out-of-pocket costs to obtain your real estate license. Here's how it works.

1. First, do a little background investigation into several real estate firms that you might like to work for, and set up an appointment with their designated broker for a meeting. It's always good to get to know those at the top, even if you decide to go with another firm. Since reputable real estate companies are always on the lookout for good agents, they will appreciate your due diligence.
2. Be prepared with a list of questions you wish to ask the designated brokers in these firms. Bear

with us; there is a reason to do this before you get your license. The following are a list of questions you should ask as you meet with the designated broker.

a. How many agents and associate brokers work here?

b. What support is given to your agents? (Signage? Business Cards? Lock Boxes & Access? Office Space & Equipment?)

c. What is expected of your agents? (Phone time? Weekly Office Meetings?)

d. What is your commission structure? (Transaction Fees? Commission Splits? 100% Options?)

e. Is the designated broker a working broker? Here's what is meant by that—do they current help clients buy and sell properties? The reason this can be important is that brokers who are active agents will sometimes not have the time to give you the help you need as a new agent because they are working their own business as well. Also, when calls come into the office, they will take the cream of the crop for themselves, and you will not get walk-in traffic.

f. How do they handle walk-in prospects or phone requests? For example, if someone calls on one of your listings, is that call given directly to you? Or, do they give it to the agent doing phone time? This can be critical to a new agent who needs the "up" calls from their listing signs.

g. Do they have a spouse or other relative who works in the office? This is also imperative. If they do, you can bet that family member or spouse will receive most of the "up" calls and walk-in business.

h. Do they reimburse for school and licensing fees? (make this the last question on your list.)

There are many other things you'll need to discover about how the firm of your choice works, but we'll be going over those in a later chapter. For now, these are some of the questions to ask as you interview the firms you have on your list. Finding a job with a real estate company is much different than any other position or career for which you'll ever interview. Here's why! You are in charge. You will be working as an independent contractor, which is like running a business within a business. You'll be interviewing them as much as they will you.

State Licensing Requirements

Most states require you to be at least 18 years old because that is the legal age to enter a legal and enforceable agreement. Since you will be the authorizing agent on listing and purchase agreements, you must meet the legal age requirement. Although you do not need any specific education other than a high school degree, most states require a certain number of hours in real estate specific education. Since the number of real estate educational hours can differ from state to state, you'll need to look online or contact the Department of Real Estate to discover the required hours for your state.

Most states require approximately 90 hours of course work from an accredited real estate school or university; online courses are not acceptable. For those of you who will not be reimbursed from a chosen real estate firm, expect to pay around $250 and then you'll need to get fingerprinted, which will cost about $25 to perform the fingerprints and another $70 for a Clearance Card from the Department of Public Safety.

There are many locations in every city to be fingerprinted; just look up the location nearest you. Once you have obtained your fingerprints, they will send clearance back to you in 6-8 weeks. Clearance Cards are usually valid for six years. So, as you come to the end of your coursework, you'll want to get the fingerprinting underway. Some schools provide fingerprint services during your enrollment, at a cost that is significantly less–and, they will usually accept cash or check. It is much more efficient and convenient to get your fingerprinting done at the school.

After each class is completed, you will receive a certificate. After receiving all the certificates for your courses, you will be asked to show all your certificates of completion to take your school's final exam. To qualify for the state exam, most schools require that you pass the school exam with a score of 80 percent or higher.

The time it takes to complete the course work differs for every student. Some go to both day and evening classes to finish within a few weeks. Others are not able to take a rush course, and it takes six to eight weeks or more to complete.

Living in a bigger city offers more opportunities for course work, enabling some over-achievers to get their classroom hours completed within 8-10 days. However, other states will not allow any more than 9 credit hours to be taken per day, which means your required hours could take you months to complete. Similar to the state exam, the school exam will usually consist of 200 multiple choice questions, to include both state and national policies and laws.

Then you'll need to schedule your state exam, which is only offered at pre-scheduled times. You might have to wait several weeks before you can take your state test. Schools often admit that the school test is more challenging for students than the state exam. This might be so that they can assure themselves that you are more than ready to take and pass the state assessment, especially since you'll be required to pay each time you test for the state. The cost in most states is approximately $75, and they will usually not accept a personal check. It will need to be paid by money gram or money order; however, check again for your state's requirements.

Once you have completed all your courses and passed your school exam, you will need to arrive at least 30 minutes early to your testing site and have the following information available.

- A Prelicensure Education Certificate form that has been received from the school you attended.

- Two forms of identification with your legal name being the same name as on your certificate and fingerprint card. One of your forms of identification must be government issued and contain a photo. The other can be a signed credit or debit card or your social security card with your signature.

- You will need a four-function calculator for the math portion of your exam.

- You will also need to have your register confirmation number to prove to the examiner that you were scheduled for that date and time. If you fail to bring all the necessary forms, certificates, identifications and other required documents with you, most states will count that as a missed appointment, and you will forfeit your fee.

- If you have an emergency and need to reschedule your exam, you will need to do that at least three days in advance or forfeit your fee. When you reschedule your exam, you will be asked to pay $75 test fee once again.

You will receive confirmation that you have passed or failed your state test immediately after taking the exam. Once you have passed your state exam, you'll need to then apply with the state for your license. Getting your license is usually done at your state Department of Real Estate location. The following is what will be needed to be licensed.

- Salesperson application and fee
- Prelicensure Education Certificate that you received from the school you attended
- State exam score report that you received from the state upon taking your state exam
- Proof of legal presence
- Original Licensure Questionnaire
- Copy of your Clearance Card (front & back)
- Course completion hours certificates
- A hiring form provided by your broker (get from broker or online—must be signed by broker)
- License fee (usually about $50)
- Real Estate Recovery Fund fee of $10

Most Department of Real Estate offices are not open on the weekends but check with your individual state departments.

Setting Realistic Expectations

Since you will be writing and authorizing legal agreements that will involve millions of dollars throughout your real estate career, the requirements and exams can be demanding. Don't be surprised or disappointed if you don't pass the school or state exams the first time you take them. They can be complicated and confusing, and even the brightest, most successful Realtors® did not pass the exams on their first attempts. The score you make on the exam in no way is an indicator of how successful you will be as a real estate agent.

You will be told this many times as you go through real estate school and take the state exam, but it bears repeating here. The school is to prepare you to pass the state exam. Some information is helpful and necessary, and some information you might rarely use in your real estate career. So, work through the process of getting your license one step at a time. Let's review the steps.

1. Interview local real estate firms in which you might be interested in working.

2. Find an accredited real estate school to take your course work (approximately 90 hours).

3. Get fingerprinted, and send your card to the Department of Public Safety for your Clearance Certificate.

4. Take your school exam.

5. Take your state exam.

6. Take all documents into the Department of Real Estate for licensing.

Instead of waiting until you have completed all your classwork and exams, you might want to begin thinking about what type of real estate you want to sell. What do you think will be an area or niche that best suits you? For example, if you know a lot about horses and horse facilities, you may want to represent clients looking for horse property or land investments. If you have an educational background, you may want to focus on a particular area where you are familiar with the school district. Perhaps you want to sell in your neighborhood and become known as the recognized expert in your community. You may not have a niche, as yet, and that's understandable. The longer you practice real estate, the closer you will get to identifying the area of sales that you enjoy the most and where you can be the most effective.

Before striking out on your own, you might find it more appealing to work as a buyers' agent for a listing agent within the office you have chosen. Or, you may decide to team up with other agents and work together to provide that added touch of service for your prospects that will position you above many newbies in your market. There are many opportunities as a new real estate agent, so be sure to investigate which ones are available and appealing as you plan your career path. We'll be covering some of these options as we get further into the book.

Think of your new career as a living, growing, ever-changing entity that has many facets to explore and expand your real estate vision. The career path you first choose as a new real estate agent might change significantly as your knowledge and skills mature. The beauty of being a real estate agent is that your success is not limited to your years in the business. Many new agents have become multi-million dollar producers their first year in the industry, and many others have spent a decade in real estate, with nothing much to show for their efforts but yearly dues and business costs being taken out of their bank accounts. The ladder usually loses interest and income because they failed to continue their education and apply all the resources offered to them. Make up your mind today that you are not going to be one of those type agents.

What's the Difference Between a Realtor® and an Agent?

Although we will talk about the different designations and affiliations in a later chapter, one of the most important things you can do as a new real estate agent is join the National Association of Realtors® (®NAR). You'll also want to become a member of your local Board of Realtors®, which is determined by the area or areas in which you want to transact business. The ®NAR is the largest trade association in the United States, and your membership dues each year will be about $120. To become a member of a local Board of Realtors® will be an additional fee, and they are all different depending on the local area.

Along with being a Realtor® is the prestige and power these organizations have in local and national policies and legislation. When you have a voice in your local and national boards, you can help form laws and make reforms that will directly affect how you and your associates conduct business. Realtors® get a lot of information about new market trends, and they offer continued education and annual renewal hours that can be more available and affordable to their members.

Finally—education completed, exams are taken and passed, real estate firm chosen, and you're ready to go out there and make a million, right? Well, not so fast. There is much to learn along the way, so keep reading as you're working.

Chapter 2: Five Activities Your First Five Weeks in the Business

The first five weeks in the real estate business will be quite busy, even though you may not have many listings or be working with many buyers yet. The following five activities are what should be consuming your time for the first five weeks as a new Realtor®. The more thoroughly you do these first five activities, the stronger foundation you will have on which to build your business.

Activity #1—Communicate to your Sphere of Influence

You are excited about starting a new chapter in your life—about building a career in real estate. One of the first things to do is make a list of everybody you know. This will be the beginnings of a business database, so include as much information as possible. If you are using program manager software, you can create groups for your people to make it easier to market to them later. Hopefully, you'll have names, addresses, phone numbers, email addresses, and social media sites for everyone on your list.

When you first sit down to list all those that will form your database, you think there won't be very many people, but the list will expand when you allow your mind to explore your sphere. Here are some of the areas you will find people to form your sphere of influence.

- Friends & Family
- Former Co-workers
- Neighbors
- Club Members and Affiliates
- Other Hobby Enthusiasts
- Church Members
- People from the Dog Park
- Attendees at Your HOA Meetings
- PTA Parents
- Teachers
- Children's Friend's Parents
- Old School Classmates
- People on Your Sports Team
- Doctors, Dentists, Lawyers & Other Professionals
- Your Car Mechanic
- Contacts in Your Outlook Program
- Friends on Social Media

These are just a few of the obvious places to find those to put on your list. Ask other agents in your office who they first put on their sphere of influence lists. Your database should be revised every week to keep it current. As you are creating your initial list, try to get 100 people and their complete contact information.

Once you have their information, send an announcement to those in your database telling them about your new career in real estate. Some you may want to send out as direct mail pieces, and some you can email. Be sensitive to those on your list who may not be tech-savvy, and make sure you contact them by snail mail or email. Reserve your texts, or social media contacts for those whom you know are on their sites every day.

With every contact on your list, be sure to include a call to action. Don't just tell them you are now selling real estate for ABC Realty located at ________. Let your words show them how excited you are to be a Realtor®. Your brokerage might already have pre-designed announcement cards to be sent to your sphere of influence, and they might also have an email form of the announcement. If not, then you'll need to write the message yourself. It could read something like this.

Hi Donna, I'm so excited to let you know that I just got my real
estate license and am now working with ABC Realty. Keep me
in mind when it comes time to buy or sell your home. I'd love to
share your experience and help you find the perfect place for you
and your family. Give me a call; I'll let you know about our new
XYZ program; I think it would be perfect for you.

Don't forget to include your contact information, business card, company logo and any information required by your designated broker. It's always a good idea to have your broker look over any communications you plan to send to be sure you are compliant with company and state requirements. Your broker will also be able to share what others in the office have done, and give you some great ideas for your ongoing communications to make them more enticing and informative.

Activity #2—Adopt a 5 x 5 Plan

Here's what a 5 x 5 plan looks like. Do the follow five activities five days a week.

1. Pass out your business card to five new contacts, five days a week. (Pass them out to people in restaurants, grocery stores, at the mall, etc.)

2. Communicate with five friends or family members about real estate five days a week. (Make a phone call, send a personal note or card to let them know you were just thinking about them.)

3. Make five cold calls each day for five days a week. (Get the numbers off For Sale by Owners in your Farm area.)

4. Write five personal notes each day for five days a week. (These can be placed on For Sale by Owner's doors, your Farm area doors, etc.)

5. Contact five other realtors a day for five days a week. (these can be in person in your office, or by email, Facebook, LinkedIn, Twitter, etc.)

Activity #3—Get Active on Social Media Sites

Your real estate company will probably already have your photo and any listings you have on their website, but it's a good idea to have your personal website as well. You can include so much more information. Shop other Realtors® sites and see how they have designed them and what they have included that appeals to you. Some of the things you should include on your website are as follows.

- Home search that keeps them on your site. (dslDXpress)
- Market Trends
- Agent and Company Information
- Community Information & Events
- Neighborhood Sales and Listings
- Testimonials
- Your Listings & Sales (you may not have any of these at first)
- Monthly Newsletter (your company may already have a template you can use)
- Current Personal Photo
- Current Mortgage Rates or Mortgage Calculator
- Mortgage & Title People You Plan on Using

Begin establishing a community on Twitter and LinkedIn as well. Not only will you make a lot of business contacts, but you'll learn from other professionals.

Activity #4—Choose a Farm Area

Farm areas for Realtors® can be selected by specialty or location, whichever works best for your goals and plan. For example, if you decide to specialize in luxury homes, or horse properties, or lawyer contacts, or military people—whomever you feel you might already have an in with, that could be your farm. Or, you can choose a location to farm. It could be your neighborhood or a part of the city or town with which you are very familiar. Eventually, you may have several farms, but at this early stage, it's best to focus on just one.

You farm is where you harvest most of your business, where you focus much of your efforts so that you can dominate that marketplace. Claim your farm—own it, and refuse to let any other Realtor® have a stronghold in your farm area. There's a way to go about doing that, and we'll talk about that when we cover marketing yourself and your properties.

A word of caution, if you choose to make your farm upper-end, luxury homes, know that you will have a tremendous amount of competition from very experienced Realtors®. They too are after the lion's share of commissions, but it doesn't mean that you can't be successful. That's the beautiful thing about real estate, all things are possible. You can take that last statement to the bank—ALL THINGS ARE POSSIBLE!

Activity #5—Attend Ongoing Real Estate Training

You've just gotten out of school, and the last thing you want to do right now is set through more training, but it's important to continue your education. Because the real estate industry is always changing, you need to keep up with the times. Your education doesn't always mean sitting through a lecture or hearing a speaker. Here is a list of things that will contribute to your knowledge of today's real estate market.

- Take a top producer in your office out to lunch and encourage them to share their story of how they continue to out-perform others in the industry.

- If your office has other offices in the city, ask the designated broker of another office if you can attend their office meeting. It will give you fresh ideas of how others have created their successes.

- Develop strong relationships with several title officers from different companies. Good title people will prove invaluable when it comes to processing challenging contracts. Ask other top producers who they recommend for their title work. They'll have some great resources for you.

- Meet with a few mortgage loan officers as well. They will give you wonderful ideas for how to help your clients get qualified. Nurture these relationships; you'll need their help as you build your career. Many of them will also return the favor, sending you referrals and keeping you abreast of what's going on in the lending world.

- Read books written by real estate leaders, or listen to them on tape in your car when you are going to and from appointments. You will be amazed at all the information they will share with you. Be like a sponge and soak up all their knowledge.

- Attend training when national speakers come into town. Decide you are going to be a student of real estate throughout your entire career. Remember to return the favor as you mature in your career and a newbie in the industry asks for advice from you. Pay it forward; be patient and kind to those who are just starting out in real estate.

- Read ads, newsletters, publications, emails, and examine the social media sites of others in the industry to get to know what your competition is doing. Knowing your competition is invaluable. Not only will you learn what works, but you also learn what doesn't work, and you'll most likely save yourself a lot of money in the process.

If you can do all these things the first five weeks, you will be well on your way to becoming a top-producing Realtor®. Try not to focus on how many sales you need to have in a month or a year, or how many listings, or how many buyers you need to work with this week. That will only frustrate you. Instead, just focus on doing these five activities, and you will be rewarded with sales success and ongoing job satisfaction.

When You Suffer Setbacks

You can do all these things and still experience few rewards at first. That's the downside to being a Realtor®. Sometimes it seems like all your hard work is for nothing—there's just nothing happening, no responses that are bringing you income. Keep on working hard. When things begin to happen, it usually happens all at once. One month there's nothing, and the next month you don't have time to take a breath.

There's nothing harder than to continue to work hard when you don't see immediate results. We are a society that has been conditioned to everything being instant. However, real estate doesn't work that way. It takes time to build your business. If it were as easy as working hard and having everything you do bring business, there wouldn't be enough business for all those who would want to become Realtors®.

You're going to have disappointments and setbacks, but those don't have to be career stoppers. Being successful doesn't mean you never experience negatives, it's how you handle those negatives that swing the pendulum from average to outstanding. If you want to become an excellent agent, you'll need to persevere. You can allow yourself about ten whole seconds to pout or wallow in self-pity but refuse to turn a 10-second pity party into weeks of depression. The same holds true for successes. Agents who experience early success can mistakenly think this business is easy-peasy, and celebrate their success until they find their pipeline of business and their pocketbooks empty. Reward yourself for success, but don't turn it into a three-week unproductive laze around.

Celebrating Your Successes

It's also good to reward your efforts, even when you haven't yet hit pay dirt. Early success might mean you have completed all your activities for a week. That's achievement. Success might mean that you faced your fears and stepped outside your comfort zone to try a new approach. That's achievement. Success might mean you learned and applied a new strategy. That's achievement. During the first few weeks of your real estate career, accomplishments are going to be recognized for your efforts—not necessarily by the responses you receive.

To encourage yourself to continue to practice your 5 x 5 plan, reward yourself. Take you and your significant other out to a sporting event, or take an afternoon and go to a movie. Don't make every waking hour all about real estate. Keeping a balance is unbelievably important. Real estate can take its toll on personal relationships, especially when you are a rookie. Think about it! You're gone a lot trying to build your business. You're probably experiencing some mood swings as you work hard and yet aren't making any money. You could be putting a financial strain on your family. There are a lot of contributors that can stress out your romantic relationship. So, be aware of these things, and try hard to preserve a balance in your career. Show your spouse or significant other your appreciation for their support, and you love for their understanding.

A good way to get them aboard your new career is to involve them in the early stages of planning. Talk about how you're going to build your business, and solicit their help. Involve them in your celebrations as well. Talk about your dreams, about what you're going to do to reward yourself and your family when you make your first benchmark or goal. Let them share in the excitement, and they'll be much more open to making some temporary sacrifices.

Don't wait to begin doing these activities, begin today. Continue to use this book as a guideline for success, but act today, so you stay on the success track. Start working on your sphere of influence this very evening so that tomorrow you can begin your 5 x 5 activities.

Chapter 3: Keys to the Listing Appointment

Many new Realtors® chose to focus on buyers when they first begin their real estate careers. While it's true buyers are easier to find, they are also easier to lose. You may make more immediate money working with buyers at first, but the real money in real estate is with listing properties. Listings are your inventory. Once you've done your initial call for the appointment, created your listing package, made the listing presentation, and put your signage up, you can get on to the next listing. Your focus should be on obtaining saleable listings, and no matter what you may think—there's a buyer for every home.

If you have enough listings, you'll have more than your fair share of buyers. In fact, you'll learn that the best policy is to refer the buyers to other agents, let them find them a home and pay you a referral fee, and simply keep on building your inventory of listed homes. There will be some that you won't want to refer, but most of your time should be spent actively pursuing listings. So, let's examine the best ways to go about getting the listings as a new agent. Obviously, you are going to have a lot of competition, so you'll need to have a plan up your sleeve to capture the lion's share of the business.

Some of the following five key points to get listings will force you to think like an entrepreneur, so don't fear to be different. Make sure that anything including in your real estate toolbox that is out of the norm is approved ahead of time by your broker. There's nothing more embarrassing than promising a prospect you can do something special for them that your broker opposes. Keep in mind, anything creative you wish to offer your prospects to help you attain the listing must be legal and ethical.

Five Key Points to Getting the Listing Appointment

Key #1: Put together a listing presentation package.

You do not have to reinvent the wheel when you create a presentation package. Whether you use your laptop to create an online presentation, or you give your prospects a paper presentation binder, have both types of the presentation ready to use immediately. A quick way to put together a presentation is to ask your broker what he or she would recommend being included and use what others have already put together. The only thing that will be different is your comparable property information, your cover photo and listing address, your contact and personal information, and some of the special plans you might have put together for your sellers. If your broker has nothing to share with you regarding a listing presentation package, then make sure it includes the following.

- A photo of the seller's home at the beginning of the presentation. Put this on a disk, and offer it to the sellers for allowing you to meet with them; they'll appreciate the gesture.

- A group of comparable homes that have sold in the area over the past 3-6 months. Include the MLS listing that shows the features, listing price, selling price, and date the home sold. The date can be extremely valuable to sellers. They want to get their home sold as quickly as possible for the highest price. If some sold for higher than you are recommending, make sure you point out the days on the market.

- An estimated cost sheet should be included in your presentation package. This will let the sellers know approximately how much they can expect to make if their home sold for the price you are recommending. Get a mortgage flyer from the loan officer you have established a relationship with, and have information about their mortgages with current interest rates available in your presentation package.

- An information sheet about how to properly prepare or stage their home for a quick sale at the highest price possible. This sheet should educate the sellers about how to prepare their home to be shown in its best possible light.

- A marketing plan you have designed specifically for them, listing step-by-step how you plan to make sure their home gets maximum exposure to every agent and buyer in the city.

- A seller's expectation sheet. This lets the sellers know what they can expect from you within the first 24-hours after you have listed their home. It lets them know that you are going to be actively pursuing buyers and promoting their home.

- Agent's expectation sheet. This informs the sellers what they will need to do to keep their home in top-of-the-market condition for a quick sale.

Key #2: Make the call to get the listing.

There are many things you can do to convince them you are the right agent to help them sell their home, but you cannot do this over the phone. All the phone call is for is to get the listing appointment. To do that, you need a plan that includes a unique offering that others are not doing. The following is just one idea, but when you come up with your plan, be sure to obtain your broker's approval before making any promises to the sellers.

- Create a selling partnership. Let sellers know they could sell their home through you and receive full service on their listing, including MLS, advertising, everything for only $1,000 (or whatever figure in which you and your broker agree). This is going to get the attention of the sellers, and they will immediately begin asking your questions. Let them know that's what you'd like to talk to them about, then let them know you have some free time this afternoon at 2:00 or 4:00. Which time would be better for them? Avoid asking a yes or no response question, because it's much more likely the seller's first response will be "no." For example, don't ask if you can drop by this afternoon and present your program to them.

Persistent sellers will continue to ask more information about your program. Make an excuse to get off the phone. You can even start the phone call with the fact that you have another appointment in just a few minutes that is close to them, and while you're in the area you could come by to explain your program at 2:00 or 4:00. Which time would work better for them?

Some sellers will ask you several times, just give them a little bit more information that peaks their interest. You could say something like, I can tell you have some experience with buyers, and that's what I'd like to talk to you about. I can show you how to pay a flat fee of only $1,000, and yet reap all the benefits of having a full-service Realtor® represent you.

If the seller continues, let them know you'll need to go to your appointment, but you'd love to drop by for just five minutes and explain how the program works. At this point, if they are still on the phone, they're going to be willing to give you five minutes of their time.

- Here's how the program works. Sellers will hold their own open houses. All buyers who tour the home will need to sign a Tour Sheet. The sheet will ask the buyer's name and phone number and the name of the agent with whom they are working. If the buyers are not being represented by a buyer's agent, and they want to purchase the seller's home, you agree to do the paperwork for a flat fee of $1,000. If the buyer is not represented by an agent, and is not interested in purchasing their home but is looking for a home, the sellers will call you with their names and contact information so you can follow up with them.

Most brokers should be okay with this idea, because we all know that open houses rarely sell to those who tour them. But the offering can be quite attractive to sellers, and give you an edge with the listing appointment. If you or another agent sells their home, they are responsible for paying the full commission. In working this plan, you and your sellers become true marketing partners.Avoid explaining your entire plan over the phone. Remember, this is to get the sellers' attention and entice them into giving you a listing appointment. Whatever plan you develop, you should be able to explain it quickly without giving away the farm. It should not be a gimmick, but something that is truly a win/win for everyone.

Key #3: The Listing Appointment

Show up 20 minutes early for the appointment, and call them when you arrive outside to let them know if they see a stranger outside, it's only you taking a look around their home to get a better idea of its value. One of the biggest mistakes a new real estate agent makes is to rush the listing appointment. Avoid going right in the home and sitting at the table to present your plan. Instead, comment on how nicely their home will show and ask if they'll take you for a tour. Most sellers have no objection to doing so; they are anxious to talk about their home and see what you think it is worth.

Ask their permission to take some notes on your tour. As they tell you about their home, take some notes to be used in your description for ads later—after you get the listing. That's an important point; always assume the sale—or in this case, that you will get the listing appointment. If the selling don't say much about their home, be prepared to ask some questions to open up the conversation. Ask them what made them purchase the home? What do they love most about their home? What is the one main feature they think will be most attractive to today's buyers? How have they marketed their home, so far? Use this touring time to begin to develop a relationship with the sellers. Remember, people buy from those they like, so it's your job to get them to buy into the idea of listing their home with you.

Once you have toured the home, sit with them and explain your unique program. Be ready to answer any questions and objections they may have, and move forward. Show them your listing presentation package, complete with what homes have sold for in the area. Sellers are usually very interested in that information. Then ask the question—"How can I help you get your home sold in the quickest amount of time for the highest price?" Remember, no yes or no response questions. Let them say how they believe you can get this done. Once you have written the listing agreement, leave as quickly as possible. Turn to the sheet in the listing package that lets the sellers know what to expect within the next 24-hours, and then leave as soon as possible. Don't give them time to change their minds.

Key #4: Deliver What You Promise

Make sure you do what you have told the sellers they can expect from you. If they have agreed to have a lockbox on the property and a sign outside, then make sure you have told them when they could expect those things to be done. Let them know when it will go into the Multiple Listing Service and then deliver a copy of the MLS listing for their approval. Bring a copy of the flyers you plan to put outside or pass out to neighbors and other Realtors®. Make sure they sign off on anything you design or any changes made to the MLS listing. Keep in touch, and continue to build a good relationship with the sellers.

Hold them to their agreement as well. Deliver the open house signs and ask them when they are planning to hold their first open house. Give them a welcome sheet for the buyers to sign, and some cards and flyers to keep for their open houses. Once you have talked to the buyers who have toured their home, keep in touch by email and communicate their comments. This will let the sellers know you are working hard for them.

Key #5: Revisit the Listing

The first few weeks a house in on the market are the most critical. Hopefully, you have explained to the sellers that the longer a home stays on the market, the lower its perceived value and the less money they are likely to be offered. If there is little activity or interest, and you have been diligently working the property, it's time for a price adjustment. Obviously, this will not be the sellers' favorite topic, but it's a conversation that might save them money in the long run. The longer they postpone the inevitable, the less money they will get. Do another Market Analysis to show them any new comps in the area, and then have an honest discussion about price and value.

If you suspect the reason for a slow sale is price, you may have to take them by some of the homes in the neighborhood and show them their competition. However, if the problem is not price, you might also need to have a serious talk about the appearance of the home or how it should be staged to appeal to more buyers. If the home is priced right and looks great, there is no reason it shouldn't be getting interest and offers.

There is nothing more frightening than your first listing appointment. It is hard to act confident when your legs have turned to Jell-O, and your tongue is tied in a thousand knots. Remember this; even top producers were frightened when they toured their first home and wrote their first listing agreement. Practice what you want to say.

Got through your presentation package with a friend or family member until you are sure of what you want to say during the presentation. When you have drilled and practiced the information so much that the words come automatically to you, you're ready to present a professional listing package and write up your first listing agreement. While you're out there getting more listings, the buyers will be calling into your office, and you'll be referring them to other agents and collecting referral fees. Everybody wins!

Chapter 4: Working as a Buyers' Agent

While most top producers agree that it is much more profitable to be a listing agent, some Realtors® prefer working with buyers. The best thing to do as a new agent is to do both and see what you enjoy the most, or, who knows, perhaps you would like to work on the selling and the buying end of things. Being a buyer's agent brings with it a whole other set of strategies, skills, and issues. Let's examine what will help you obtain buyers and maintain excellent working relationships. You've already learned how to attract a bounty of buyers, but what do you do with them once they begin calling on your listings? If you have a plan as you work with your buyers, it will save you an incredible amount of time and money. The following are seven steps to practice when working with buyers.

Step #1: Always Pre-qualify Your Buyer

Even before you begin asking what buyers are looking for in a home, the first thing you need to do is be sure they can afford one.

One of the most common issues new agents have when showing homes to buyers is that they find the perfect home, only to discover that the buyers have no money, no down payment, no credit, and no viable way to purchase the home. Meanwhile, as a buyer's agent, you've just spent days of your time and a lot of money touring homes for nothing. The first question to ask buyers is how they plan on paying for the home? If they say they will be getting a loan, then your next question will be "Have you been in touch with a mortgage company?"

If they don't have a mortgage company or loan officer, feel free to give them some names and numbers. You should have at least three lenders you can recommend. Give your buyers the lenders' cards, and have them call for an appointment. Let your buyers know that it's to their benefit to line up their loan before going out there to look at homes and be disappointed when they are unable to qualify for the home in which they have fallen in love. Better to show them homes they will love and can afford. Give them your contact information, and let them know as soon as you hear from the lender telling you the amount for which they qualify, you'll set up a tour of homes to fit their needs.

If your buyers bulk at pre-qualifying, then you'll need to go on to the next buyers. Never, never waste your time driving buyers around who have not been pre-qualified.

If you want to establish some rapport with the buyers before sending them off to be qualified, then ask them what they are looking for in a home. Take notes, and then as soon as they have shared that information, say "I have a couple of homes that I believe would be perfect for you that have just come on the market. They are priced below market value, so I think they're going to go fast. I'll tell you what. Get with your lender ASAP, and I'll make some calls to see if the homes are still available."

Doing this will create some urgency with your buyers. You have peaked their interest to tour the homes you have in mind, so they are more likely to call the lenders right away. The reason for giving the buyers three names of lenders is so that you cannot be accused of steering, as well as it offers your buyers a choice of officers, different programs, and several locations from which to choose.

Step #2: Use a Buyer's Agent Agreement

This is almost as important as having your buyers' prequalified. A buyer's agent agreement lets everybody know what to expect. It clarifies that you will work hard for them, and that, in turn, they will use you exclusively to help them find a home. It's important to make it clear to the buyer that a buyer's agreement costs them nothing, but that it lets you know that you will get paid for all your hard work if they should purchase a home you have shown them. You would be hard put to find an agent who hadn't shown a gazillion homes to picky buyers only to have them go to a new home community and buy a home using the builder's agent.

When you have a buyer's agreement, you will still get paid your commission. And, your buyers will understand that you can still work for them if they decide to purchase a new build, and in fact negotiate the price for a more comfortable and profitable buying experience for them. Presented positively, most buyers will agree to authorize the agreement. Be reasonable, and don't fax an agreement to buyers before you get a chance to meet them. Spend some time with them; meet at your office and spend some time finding out what they are looking for in a home. Build rapport with them—be likable. Then, when they are comfortable with the job you will do for them, they will be much more open to authorizing a Buyer's Agent Agreement.

If you are acting as a dual agent, you will need to have an agreement for dual agency authorized by your buyers and sellers. It's also important that you are clear with your buyers that as a dual agent you cannot help them negotiate the price or give them any advice about what to offer. That would go against the fiduciary duty you owe to the sellers.

Step #3: Know Your Purchase Agreement Inside and Out

Since you'll be new in the business, it is of particular importance for you to know exactly how to complete a purchase agreement. Don't wait until your buyers want to put in an offer, to familiarize yourself with the agreement. In fact, one of the first things you should do is meet with your broker and ask him or her if there is any particular area or issue in the contract that you should be aware of that consistently causes problems with new agents.

In most purchase agreements, you will be asked to write in some information about your buyer's individual needs or wants. Your broker most likely has a standardized sheet that teaches you how to word common statements that buyers want to be added to the contract. Memorize those statements; it will come in handy when you make addendums or add statements to the purchase agreement.

If your broker cannot satisfy your questions, ask a top producer in your office for some assistance. There are times where a poorly worded statement added into a contract by an agent can significantly change the meaning of the agreement. Whatever your buyers wish to include in the purchase agreement should be written into the agreement. Whatever additions or exceptions they want, must be in writing.

Within 24 hours of the date on the contract, you need to collect earnest money and the purchase agreement must be deposited into an escrow account with the specified title company. Don't present the purchase agreement to sellers without including a copy of the earnest money check.

Step #4: Reviewing the Comps and Costs with Buyers

Both you and your buyers are always trying to get the lowest price possible for the home, but at times buyers can be entirely unreasonable by wanting you to present a low-ball offer. By law, you must present any and all offers, but it is well within your rights to educate the buyers as to the value of the home. Be sure to run comps on the home, and share them with your buyers.

Not only will it give them second thoughts about low-balling the sellers, but it will also protect them if the sellers are asking far too high a price for their home. Do your homework, and protect your buyers.

If buyers insist on low-balling sellers, then encourage them to give something else in return, so sellers won't just ignore their offer. For example, have a quicker close. Offer to pay the HOA fees, or split some of the title fees that would otherwise be paid by the sellers. Everything's negotiable. A word of caution about Home Owners Association (HOA) transfer fees. Before you offer to pay or split HOA fees, make sure you do so at closing. If the HOA requires transfer fees to be paid before closing, then ask the sellers to pay the fees and the buyers to reimburse their portion or all of the fees, at closing. That way, if the home does not close, the buyer won't get stuck paying all the fees. HOA transfer fees are usually non-refundable if the home does not close.
If you are ambitious, you can also ask that the seller pay the appraisal and inspection fees and reimbursed by the buyer at closing. Sellers may object, but if you don't ask, you don't get. HOA transfer fees can be quite steep, so be sure you find out how much it will cost and when it must be paid.

When your buyers sign a purchase agreement, give them an estimated cost sheet that will let them know what they will need to pay at the time of closing. Emphasize that all the figures are only estimates that are just meant to give them an idea of what they are looking at financially. They will appreciate the information; it's helpful for them to know what they'll need for a down payment, closing costs, and any additional title and insurance fees. It will also help them to estimate their monthly payment when they can add in principle, estimated taxes, and insurance.

Step #5: Reviewing the Sellers' Home Disclosure Forms

Every seller is required to disclose everything about their home by filling out a Sellers' Disclosure form. It is quite extensive, and some things on it could affect your buyers' decision to own the home. Make sure you review the sheet with them when you tour the home and have them initial a copy to be included in your purchase agreement. In most states, it is the law that the sellers and buyers initial it. If the sellers do not have a disclosure form available when you tour their home, and your buyers don't have a chance to review it before writing the purchase agreement, make your purchase agreement contingent upon review of the disclosure form.

They should also have a report from their homeowners' insurance company that states what claims have been made on the home and how they were resolved. The disclosure form will let you know what year the air conditioning unit is, the heating type and year, the roof condition and year, any pest infestations they may have had in the past, and numerous issues that might play a big part in whether your buyers decide to own the home. The insurance report will inform your buyers if the property has had any major plumbing issues or foundation problems, or any repeated issues that need to be addressed.

Step #6: Deliver Copies of Everything to Buyers

If you didn't pick this information up in real estate school, you should have—a purchase agreement is not legally binding if you have not delivered a signed copy to your buyers. It can be done electronically, but however, you decide to do it—your buyers must get a copy of all documents. The same applies with your listing agreements. Here are the people who should receive copies of your purchase agreement.

- Designated broker—he or she gets original purchase agreement
- Mortgage company—sometimes they require two copies
- Title company—one copy
- Buyers—one copy
- Agent—one copy

All copies should be signed in the appropriate places and initialed at the bottom corner of every page, including all addendums. Include a copy of the earnest money with copies of the purchase agreement, and keep a copy for yourself. If there are addendums to the agreement that come later, make sure all parties are given copies of those as well.

Step #7: Inspection Reports

The buyer has ten days to have an inspection of the property unless otherwise agreed to by both parties. It's also a good idea to have inspector's names and contact information because buyers rarely know who to go to for their inspections. Do this as soon as all parties agree to the purchase agreement, because it takes a while to have the home inspected and any required repairs completed. To be thorough, you may want to add a clause in your purchase agreement that states the agreement is contingent upon the home appraising for the asking price and upon approval of the inspection report.

Once the home inspection has been completed, you will make your request for repairs on the home, and the sellers have five days to accept or negotiate those repairs. If your buyers agree to purchase a home without an inspection, it's a good idea to have them sign an inspection waiver. Or, at least, write a letter with you and your buyers' signatures that explains that you recommended an inspection, but the buyers declined. This way you are covered should they try to come back later and make a claim about an existing problem with the home.

You will also need a termite report on the property. Don't be fooled into thinking that because the termite report showed no infestation, the property is free of termites. Termite inspectors are only required to report evidence of termites that can be seen. They do not have to remove any wood from a deck or look under wood that touches the ground. If there are railroad ties in the landscaping, known for harboring termites, they do not move or lift them to check for infestation. A house with a lot of wood touching the ground, especially in warmer climates, is an open invitation for termites. You may want to wiggle one and see what may be lurking just out of view of the inspector. Just give it a little trip over, and then glance beneath it when you put it back into place. Of course, this is impossible to do if the wood is buried far beneath the ground, but you can make your buyers aware that there could be a problem there.

If you see that you are going to be late on an inspection report or request for repairs, write an addendum to the contract and have the sellers approve it. Don't just call the other agent and let them know you'll be a few days late. Remember, non-compliance to these dates and times could give the sellers and buyers a way out, making the purchase agreement null and void.

Every purchase agreement is different, and everything that changes must have written approval from all parties. Rely on nothing unless it is in writing. Verbal agreements are not enforceable, so make sure you write down your buyers' requests and have all parties initial or sign their approval. It is common for the following items to change on a purchase agreement.

- Stated mortgage or title companies to be used
- Parties names on the Purchase Agreement can change for qualifying purposes
- Closing date
- Purchase price
- Included items such as washer/dryer/refrigerator/microwave, blinds/fans/etc.
- Time allotted for inspections and repairs.

These are just some of the everyday things that change, but everything is negotiable at any time; purchase agreements are living entities, they change and grow

with the times and parties involved. Almost anything is legal if all parties agree.
One thing you don't want to do is include any personal property and add its value to the purchase price of the home. This skews the appropriate value and could make the appraisal come in far below the asking price. Create a "Bill of Sale" for any personal property. This is especially common when purchasing a home on the lake. Many times, sellers will try to include their pontoons or boats in the purchase price.

There's a lot to digest in a purchase contract, but the more you do, the less intimidated you will be when filling them out in front of your buyers. If it helps to get you over your fears, you may want to have an associate go with you for support as you complete your first few agreements. They can just be introduced as your associate, and look over everything to make sure you have filled in everything correctly. Your broker has to sign the agreement as well, and he or she will catch anything that might need to be revised or rewritten.

So, don't let fear stand in your way. Go out there and write, write, write!

Chapter 5: Marketing Yourself in a Digital World

We live in a digital age, and Realtors® are responding to the need to optimize their business by creating an online presence. Billions of dollars are spent doing online marketing, but, unfortunately, the amount spent is disproportionate to the return you can expect. Online ads and business make up over 60 percent of the marketing expenditures; the question is, do they make close to those percentages in leads generation and converted sales? The answer is a resounding "NO."

The following example shows why digital marketing efforts are frequently not effective, even when Realtors® are spending billions to keep up with the Jones'. It's not that the business isn't there to be tapped, but, rather, that the average real estate agent is going about their online business with little forethought and fewer online skills and knowledge. The REAL

Trends 2013 Online Performance Study presented the following statistics.

- Consumers who researched online before buying 90%
- Consumers who believed they should receive a response within 15 minutes 45%
- Consumers who believed they should receive a response within 30 minutes 56%
- Consumers who said response time was vital when choosing their agent 89%
- Consumers who never got a response from websites 45%

This draws a dismal picture when it comes to website and online marketing. If your website is not professionally designed and well managed, it can do more harm than good. If you are going to have an individual website that touts your business, here are five tips for success.

1. Have a professional design it and maintain it; they know how to use the keywords that will give you the proper optimization.

2. Offer opt-in email forms to include buyer/seller guides, market trends, home staging information, property comps, and a mortgage calculator—to name a few.

3. Make your website mobile friendly, and include a "click and call" button for immediate response and maximum leads conversion.

4. Once you get a lead, practice quick follow-up. Even if prospects aren't quite ready to buy, send them periodic emails or put them on your blog's subscription list.

5. Create a blog that is client focused. Create links on your blog to your other social media sites, and make sure those sites are professional and informative.

It's not efficient or effective to send out broadcast emails to everyone on your social media sites, and it can be quite annoying to your friends who live in other states but are still bombarded by blanket communications that are irrelevant to them. If you are going to use broadcast media, group your contacts and only send to those who might be interested.

The best way to have a successful digital marketing plan is just that—have a plan! If you randomly update your website, rarely contribute informative blogs, and tweet or Facebook unprofessional communications that might put your business in a bad light, then forget about trying to have a presence on social media. You might create a presence all right, but it may not be the image you desire. If you are not interested or don't have the time to maintain a professional online presence, either hire it done or don't have one. Remember, you are branding

yourself with your online marketing efforts, whether you create a good or poor image, you will have one.
Your digital marketing should target your market, so avoid the "shotgun" approach. It doesn't work, and it can suck the life out of you when you've got a million other things to do. Nurture your online business just as you do your face-to-face or phone-in contacts. Make your prospects feel as though you have nothing else in the world to do but attend to their needs. If you flood the market with online broadcast communications, you'll get plenty of leads. However, it will be difficult to reach real buyers with dozens of people making up a toothpick brocade who rob you of your time and energy with no intentions of buying.
Email marketing can be effective and efficient if you target your market. Many Realtors® use email to send out flyers on homes that haven't even hit the market yet. It's like a private showing where they are encouraged to see your property before any others. People love to be first, and you can provide that for them. You might want to get permission from your sellers to delay putting their homes in MLS for a few days so you can hold a private showing or open house that is by invitation only, especially if it is a luxury home.
If you are implementing email marketing into your plan, be sure to write good copy to present the beautiful photos of the homes you'll be showing. We used to be such a visually-based society, but today's buyers and sellers are once again relating to the descriptive words used to showcase your properties. Your appeals to Realtors® are entirely different than that of buyers with whom you are currently working. You can speak more about commissions and offerings on flyers that are sent exclusively to other agents.

The key to any digital marketing is to be consistent in your efforts and the image you present. If you have a niche, market to that audience. Create a blog that ties in with what is being shown on your website and focuses on what you are tweeting. To perform your 5 x 5 activities and keep up with all the demands of an active digital campaign might be more than you can handle at the beginning of your new real estate career. If so, know when you need to solicit help from other professionals. Find a professional writer who can maintain your blog, and then give him or her the topics and pay them to write a month's worth of blogs for you. Let your design people make professional changes to your website. Have an assistant or a buyer's agent who can follow up with you, providing immediate responses for potential buyers. Doing everything yourself often means doing nothing well, so don't be afraid to delegate and do the things you enjoy the most and perform with excellence.

Using a CRM to Help Manage Your Business

CRM stands for Customer Relationship Management, which is software that acts like a computer assistant. CRMs used to perform like program management systems, but now they do so much more than that. A good CRM does the following.

- Provides storage for real estate files and photos and gives you easy access when designing flyers and online ads
- Helps you to schedule your activities and automatically sends out emails or correspondence

- Provide email drip marketing targeted campaigns
- Develops lead reports and tracks contacts
- Syncs with iOS devices
- Provides daily reminders of appointments, meetings, and keeps an active calendar
- Offers resources and methods for building ongoing customer relations

What used to be quite expensive, is now so affordable that even the newbie real estate agents who haven't yet made any sizeable income in the industry can afford to have a private, online assistant. You may even check with your broker; some real estate companies purchase CRMs per agent, giving you complete access at a reduced rate.

Everyone's needs and wants are different in which CRM will best suit them, so you'll need to do some research. There is also CRM software that offers a 30 to a 90-day trial period for you to analyze which software you like better than the others. If your broker doesn't use CRM, then ask a top producer in your office what software they use to manage their business. Then, give it a try.

Remember, if the online tools take you away from face-to-face activities and communications, then get some help. If you settle for less of a presence, less professionalism, less effectiveness, your year-end profits will be less as well. If you can't do something with excellence, don't do it at all. Real estate is not a halfway house to success; it's an all or nothing endeavor, with those at the top doing all they can and leaving nothing to chance. Their success is not accidental, but rather comes from a well-thought-out, active marketing plan.

Chapter 6: Become Goal-Oriented & Results Driven

Goals are greater than a want or need, they are more concrete than a hope or a dream, and they have the power to attract and acquire. What you feed becomes stronger. Focusing your mind on specific goals will make them attainable. Goals should be reasonable, but still stretch you just a tad beyond what you think you can achieve. Since most people stop working toward a goal they have achieved, a lower-level goal will mean lower-level performance. The words and structure of a goal are also keys to its achievement. After reading this chapter, you'll be able to write specific, high-level goals that encourage greater and more consistent success.

Since it's important to maintain a well-balanced lifestyle, it's necessary to set goals in all aspects of your life: professional, personal, and spiritual. If you're strong in one area but weak in the others, your performance in all sectors will be limited by your more ineffective goals. The relationship between strong and weak, positive and negative, good and bad, is that our strengths rarely overshadow our weaknesses; it's quite the opposite. Our weaknesses, the negatives in our lives will usually overpower our positives and our strengths.

If you want to reach full potential, your peak performance in real estate, it's necessary to achieve fullness in all walks of life—to embrace your inner purpose and understand the spiritual truths to which you resonate. Okay, that might sound a little "new age" for you, but what it means is that to be satisfied and happy in life really, you must be balanced. How does that happen? By setting appropriate and targeted goals in every aspect of your life.

Writing Specific Goals

General goals with no time frame are not goals at all; they are vague dreams that most likely will never come to fruition. To turn your dreams into goals, you need to follow these three simple steps.

1. Be specific about what you want to do or have, and write down when you plan on doing it or having it.

2. Your goals need to complement one another instead of one opposing another. For instance, you can have a professional goal that requires you to work 90 hours a week and a personal goal that says you will make the family your focus. Those two things don't go together. If you are working that many hours a week, work is your focus. With goals like that, work doesn't just fund your life; it becomes your life.

3. Your goals need to have a measurable result. How will you know if you have met with success if you don't know what you consider to be successful?

Here's an example of the difference between a dream and a specific goal.

Dream

I want to become a top producer in my office.

Goal

I will list over 100 homes my first 12 months in real estate by consistently performing my 5 x 5 activities.

You can turn your dreams into goals by following these five easy steps.

1. Put all your goals in writing.

2. Be specific when writing your goals, showing the "what" of your dream. In the above goal, that would be listing over 100 homes.

3. Write a time frame or deadline with every goal. The above goal's time frame is 12 months. Your goal might be every day, two times a week, etc.

4. Now you are writing the "how" of your dream. In the goal above, the "how" is the 5 x 5 activities.

5. Reward yourself for the goals you achieve. You can write this into your goal, or list it as a separate piece to your goals as you achieve each one.

Use the forms on the following pages to write down your goals and activities. Make sure to write goals in all areas of your life to remain balanced and satisfied. Don't forget to plan a reward for achieving your goal. If you fail to reward yourself for achievement, you will soon lose interest in doing well. Have you ever felt like all you do is work, go home and watch some television, go to bed, and get up the next day to start the same routine all over again? There's no enthusiasm for life when there's no reward for achieving your goals.

At first, you might set inappropriate goals—ones that are too easy or just impossible to achieve. That's okay; you'll do better with practice. Keep your goals in an achievement notebook, and when you think you aren't getting far enough in your career or personal life, look back several months at your past goals and congratulate yourself on all you've accomplished. It's a great way to inspire and motivate yourself to continue to turn your dreams into achievements.

Challenge yourself. Set goals that are a little higher than those you previously achieved. When you put specifics to your goals, you'll need to set up a step-by-step course of how you plan to achieve the goal. For example, if your goal were to list 100 houses this year, you would need to know the answers to the following questions and work the goal backward.

1. If my goal is to list 100 homes, how many homes is that a month? At least nine homes a month, right?

2. How many homes would I need to list per week to equal nine homes a month? To make my nine

homes a month goal, I would need to list two to three homes a week.

3. How many presentations would I need to do to list two to three home a week? If my performance history tells me that I get one listing from every five presentations I make, then I would need to plan on ten to fifteen presentations per week to get two to three listings.

4. How many calls or contacts would I need to make to set up fifteen appointments per week? If I got one listing appointment for every ten calls or contacts I made, then I would need to call on approximately 150 prospects per week.

Working your goal backward gives you your activity sheet for each day, week, month, and year. While reviewing your goals, your daily focus should be on the activities to achieve this aim. It's good to keep the end destination in view, but it is the specific daily, weekly, and monthly activities that will determine whether you achieve that goal within your stated deadline.
It is also easier to hold yourself accountable when you are keeping weekly activity logs. If you are lagging behind on achieving your goals, it will be easy to review your activity sheet and see where you are falling short. It is also possible that you are doing all your activities, but your benchmark estimates were off. Let's say it takes you 15 calls or contacts to get one listing

appointment; then you'll need to go back and check the numbers and perhaps adjust your deadline.

Your goals sheet and activity log should be completed for every goal. The following samples will help you keep track.

Goals Sheet

Write a general want here.

I want to (have or do) ...
____

____

What will I need to do to (have or do) this goal...
____

____

What is my deadline (date) for achievement of the goal?
____

____

Using the above information, write your specific goal statement here.

____

What are the steps I will take for achieving this goal? (this is the how of your goal)

1. ____

____

2. ____

3. ____

4. ____

5. ____

When I have achieved this goal, I plan to reward myself by...

____

Weekly Activity Sheet

DAYS	CONTACTS	APPOINTMENTS	LISTINGS	MARKETING	MANAGE
Mon.					
Tues.					
Wed.					

Thurs.					
Fri.					
Sat.					
Sun.					

You can customize this activity sheet any way that fits your goals, and use it to track your activities. The activity sheet above is designed to track how many hours you spend each day on these activities. Or, you can track your activities by the number of contacts or calls you made and the number of appointments that resulted from those calls. How many listings did you get from your efforts? What marketing methods were used to generate leads, and how did you market yourself? You broker may also have a goals and activity sheet that is better suited to your needs. At this point, the tool is not as important as the act of completing the forms so you can track your activities and their results. These forms are elementary; you can also use your CRM software to help you record and track your activities.

If you don't reach success in the first few weeks, don't give up. Keep holding your feet to the fire, and before long you'll see your success begin to build. After the first few months, go back and review your activities sheet and make adjustments on how much time you spent doing what. If you see that you are more successful doing the one activity than another, then concentrate on doing what works for you. Don't waste time trying to bring all your other activities up to average, do more of what you do best—focus on your strengths. Remember, what you feed gets stronger.

Conclusion:

The Advantages of a Career in Real Estate

As difficult as it is starting your real estate career, generating and working leads, putting together listing presentations, negotiating purchase agreements, it's incredibly rewarding when it all comes together in a successful transaction. To know you've been a part of helping others settle their families, find good schools for their children, and contribute to the community provides ongoing motivation to continue to succeed in real estate.

Although real estate is demanding, it also offers freedoms that other careers do not. You're not limited to a two-week vacation each year. Your income is what you make it. If you want a raise, you just work harder and smarter. It's especially generous for women, who can become top producers, leaders in an industry that doesn't favor men over women, and one that offers equal pay for equal effort. There is no pay difference between men and women. Everyone has an incredible opportunity to experience more success than they ever dreamed possible.

Real estate agents aren't stuck in a dead-end, go-nowhere job. Advancements are the direct result of individual merit. You are rewarded and recognized for all your hard work. You are appreciated and thanked when you help sellers get top dollar for their homes and buyers qualify for their loans. It's one of the highest paid, most enjoyed careers in today's society. Think about it! When was the last time your boss gave you a hug and told you how much he or she appreciated your help? Most successful Realtors® can answer that question quickly because it happens all the time. As an agent, you get to be the hero when you go the extra mile to help a family in need.

There is no ceiling cap to how much you can make in your real estate career. You have constant opportunities to learn and grow as you compete with top producers in the industry. There is no division between upper-management and someone two weeks into the business. You're all out there with a job to do, and on any given day, with hard work, knowledge, skills, and an attitude of selling, you can win a listing from someone who's been in the business for 20 years or more. When you do, it's such a rush!

Even when you're working on a commission split within a real estate company, you have all the perks of owning and operating a business within a business. You are independent; you get to call the shots. You can also take advantage of many of the tax benefits that entrepreneurs have available to them as they work their businesses. The difference is, you have fewer ownership worries and headaches. There's no stress over renting office space, paying utilities, or buying all the equipment and machinery of a new store front business person.

Your startup costs for a career in real estate is minimal compared to many other businesses, but your money-making potential is just as high, if not higher than most other occupations. You don't have big brother hanging over your shoulder every moment, but you get to be the recognized industry expert by your clients. It's empowering!

Real estate can be a demanding mistress, though, if you let her. She can steal the time you have with your family. She can convince you that you're just not cut out to be a real estate agent and cause you to give up just before you're about to climb the crest of the hill to cross over to greater heights of achievement. What you must do is stand your ground. Don't give up, because just when it seems the darkest; your career will take an amazing upswing. What separates the average from the over-achiever is not so much that a top producer doesn't experience failure, but that he or she doesn't let failure squelch their ability to get back up and try again.

Surround yourself with people who believe in you, who encourage you and share in your setbacks and successes. Keep studying and learning your craft, honing your skills, gaining more knowledge. Expect greatness because most of us get what we expect—the problem is we don't expect much.

Thank you for making it through to the end of *Real Estate Agent; How to Become a Successful Real Estate Agent (Volume 3)*. Let's hope it was informative and able to provide you with all the tools you need to achieve your goals, whatever they may be.

The next step is to go out there and generate leads, dominate the market, become a top producer, and pay it forward to the next newbie in your office. Adopt a "no mercy" attitude and decide that you will not give yourself a way out. You'll succeed, no matter what. When another agent beats you out of a listing, analyze what you did and try harder. Stay in touch with the sellers, not to steal the listing or interfere with the agent they are working with, but holding the position of a close second. You never know when they will need an agent, so be first in line to recapture that listing.

When you're working with buyers who don't know what they want or decide to go with another Realtor®, wish them well. Don't be shy about asking them what changed their minds. Learn from your mistakes and do better next time. Let setbacks make you stronger and sharper, and competition inspircs you to provide better customer service and unique opportunities for sellers and buyers that might never have been done before in the real estate industry. Be a creative thinker and doer, confident and assured that you're the best one to help your clients.

Picture yourself attending your company banquet or the ®NAR convention and accepting an award for being one of the top producers in the country. Nobody can hold you back except yourself, and since nobody wants you to succeed more than you—step out there and make it happen! Next year will bring new challenges and greater opportunities; be ready for them by conquering those you face today.

Thank you again for investing your time and money in purchasing this book. Finally, if you found this book useful in any way, a review on Amazon is always appreciated!

Book Description

Are you ready to begin your career in real estate? Then give yourself a kick-start in the industry by reading this book. You'll learn a step-by-step licensing process, and what comes next to bring you success as a Realtor®. Do you have questions about how to build your business? We can help with those concerns. After reading this book, you'll learn how to generate leads, create marketing plans that will help you compete with today's top producers, and know how to help sellers get the highest price for their homes.

When you study and apply our unique strategies and proven skills, you'll soon take advantage of all the opportunities the real estate industry offers. We'll teach you how to adopt the professional attitude of a top producer. Your new skills and knowledge will give you the confidence and assurance you'll need to conquer market challenges and become thc director of your professional destiny. Before long, you'll be setting a new standard of excellence, and others will be coming to you for advice and guidance.

Presented with the current management software and digital tools, you'll be able to brand yourself and create a remarkable image of success. We'll teach you how to set and attain goals you never thought possible, turning yesterday's dreams into tomorrow's reality.

CPSIA information can be obtained
at www.ICGtesting.com
Printed in the USA
BVHW081753090919
557952BV00014B/1835/P